D1859919

AN INTRODUCTION TO BALANCE SHEET AND STUDY OF FINANCIAL STATEMENTS

AN INTRODUCTION TO BALANCE SHEET AND STUDY OF FINANCIAL STATEMENTS

H.R. Gupta

KALPAZ

©Author
All rights reserved. No part of this work may be reproduced, stored, adapted, or transmitted in any form or by any means, electronic, mechanical, photocopying, micro-filming recording or otherwise, or translated in any language, without the prior written permission of the copyright owner and the publisher. The book is sold subject to the condition that it shall not, by way of trade or otherwise, be lent, resold, hired out, or otherwise circulated without the prior publisher's written consent in any form of binding or cover other than that in which it is published.

The views and opinions expressed in this book are author(s) own and the facts reported by them have been verified to the extent possible, and the publishers are not in any way liable for the same.

ISBN: 978-81-7835-990-8
Price: ₹ 835

Third Edition 2014

Published by

Kalpaz Publications
C-30, Satyawati Nagar,
Delhi - 110052
E-mail: kalpaz@hotmail.com Ph.: 9212142040
Laser Typesetting : Shah Computer Graphics
Printed at : G. Print Process, Delhi

Cataloging in Publication Data—DK
Courtesy: D.K. Agencies (P) Ltd. <docinfo@dkagencies.com>

Gupta, H.R.
An introduction to balance sheet and study of financial statements / H.R. Gupta. — 3rd ed.
p. cm.
ISBN 9788178359908

1. Banks and banking—India. 2. Financial statements—India. I. Title.

DDC 332.10954 23

Dedicated to my respected father Late Shri Keshoram Gupta, resident of Gajsinghpur (Distt. Sriganganagar), Manager, Punjab National Bank and State Bank of Bikaner and Jaipur, industrialist, businessman and social worker.

Contents

PART –2

Foreword

I have gone through the III Edition of "An Introduction to Balance Sheet and Study of Financial Statements" written by Prof. H.R. Gupta, Manager (Retd.), Punjab National Bank and find that the book is very useful for bankers, students, of commerce and finance, Articles of CA/CS, MBA, BBA, BCA, FCA courses, traders, NRIs etc. as a reference book.

In this edition the following more chapters have been added looking to their importance in the present Era:

1. Emergence of ATM in Banking Sector
2. An Era of Computerisation of Banks
3. Real Time Gross Settlement System (RTGS)
4. Trading on-line through Internet
5. Electronic-Commerce
6. Consolidation in Banks—Merger and Acquisition
7. Banking through Internet
8. Mutual Fund
9. Preventive Measures to Avoid Frauds in Commercial Banks:

   (i) Housing Loan

   (ii) ATMs.

Prof. H.R. Gupta has covered almost all topics on Banking and Finance. The efforts put in by him are appreciable.

I wish him a good health and bright future. God may bless him with happiness and long life.

Place: Bikaner
Date: 22.12.12

Gauri Shankar Khatri
B.Com, CAIIB
Ex-Manager,
State Bank of Bikaner and Jaipur
Counseller Financial Literacy and
Credit Counselling Centre
Bikaner-334001 (Raj.)

Preface to the 3rd Edition

The 2nd edition of the book was published in the year 2005 and sold out in a very short period, there was big demand for the revised 3rd edition. So, I had to go for the 3rd edition of the book which is in your hands.

The book is divided into four parts. I have added two new chapters in part 1st namely:

1. Depreciation 2. Bank Reconciliation.

In the part 2nd the new chapters are: 1. Preventive measures to avoid frauds of ATMs in PSB, 2. Preventive measures to avoid housing loan frauds in PSBs.

In part 3rd the new chapters included are: 1. Non-Resident Accounts 2. Small Industries Development Bank of India (SIDBI) 3. Corporate Governance in Public Sector Banks.

I have also introduced part 4th consisting of the following chapters:

1. Electronic commerce -Application in Banking Sector.
2. Real Time Gross Settlements System (RTGS)
3. Consolidation in banks through merger and acquisitions.
4. Trading online through Internet.

5. Emergence of ATM in Banking sector.
6. An era of computerisation of Banks.
7. Banking through Internet.
8. A few challenges before banking sector.
9. A Sea-change in Banking sector in India after Independence.

I have tried to give maximum to the readers-in India and abroad in this 3rd edition. The book is of immense use for bankers at all levels, students of commerce and finance, Articles of C.A CS courses, MBA students, Traders, NRIs, Exporters/Importers as a reference book.

Any suggestion for the improvement in the quality, and utility of the book is welcome.

Acknowledgements

I am thankful to my wife Smt. Urmila Gupta M.A.B.Ed. who has inspired me and given me all kind of help and assistance in the publication of this edition. I am also thankful to my son Mr. Deepak Gupta B.E. (working as SDE in BSNL, Bikaner) who helped me in typing the matter of the book in a very short period and friends and relatives for necessary help and guidance.

Author

A Penny Spent on Books is an Investment because:
Books are the food for youth;
the delight of old age;
the ornament of prosperity;
the refuse and comfort of adversity;
a delight at home, and no hinderance abroad;
companions by night, in travelling, in the country.

Books are keys to wisdom's treasure;
Books are gates to lands of pleasure;
Books are paths that upward lead;
Books are friends, come, let us read.

Every single penny invested in a book is a very fine and enduring investment. Humanity would be infinitely poorer from every point of view had it not been for great books that have nourished and nurtured human civilisation down through the ages.

H.R. Gupta

Banking

Mobilise deposits with earnest zeal
Deploy credit with CDR feel
Remember triad 'Safety' 'liquidity'
And 'Profitability'
'Business' is possible through staff productivity
Ancillary business may be a squirrel's share
Foreign exchange is there as a top gear
Profit is cause, effect and result of business
Profitability is the lever to achieve success
If 'business' is forewheel
Administrator the 'rear' one
Remember it is the rear wheel that generates power
And only a clean engine can generate power
Harnessing of material, monetary and manual resources
Is the other name of any 'Business'
Keep the material clean and neat with decoration
May it be premises, furniture, Accounts or Reconciliation
Security, Profitability and Productivity are the
Peculiarities of monetary resource
'Recycling' of funds is a paramount force
Manual resource is the kingpin

Of the whole mechanism
It can be lubricated/activated
Only by motivation.
MIS are the arteries and veins of the organization
Systems and Procedures the backbone
Earnest desire for knowledge and firm determination
The source to strengthen them alone.
By M.B.Vaishnav
Adapted from IBA Bulletin, Oct., 1992.

PART – I

PART – I

1

Introduction—Credit Finance by Commercial Banks

Lending of funds to constituents, mainly traders, business and industrial enterprises, constitute the main business of a banking company. The major portion of bank's funds is employed by way of loans and advances, which is most profitable employment of funds. The major part of a bank's income is earned from interest and discount on the funds so lent.

The business of lending, nevertheless, is not free from certain inherent risks. Largely depending on the borrowed funds, a banker can not afford to take undue risks in lending. While lending his funds, a banker, therefore, follows a very cautious policy and conducts his business on the basis of well-known principles of sound lending in order to minimise the risks.

General Principles of Sound Lending

1. Safety, 2. Liquidity, 3. Profitability, 4. The purpose of the loan, 5. The principle of diversification of risks, 6. National policy and objectives.

1. Safety. As the banker lends the funds entrusted to it by the depositors, the first and foremost principle of lending is to ensure the safety of the funds lent. By safety is meant that the borrower is in a position to repay the loan, alongwith interest according to the terms of the loan agreement. The repayment of the loan depends upon the borrower's (i) capacity to pay and (ii) willingness to pay. The former depends upon his tangible assets and the success of his business; if he is successful in his efforts, he earns profit can repay loan promptly with certainty. Otherwise the loan is recovered out of the sale proceeds of the sale of tangible assets. The willingness to pay depends upon the honesty, character and reputation of the borrower. The banker should, therefore, take utmost care in ensuring that the enterprise or business for which a loan is sought is sound one and the borrower is capable of carrying it out successfully. He should be a person of integrity, good character and reputation. In addition to above the banker generally relies on the security of tangible assets owned by the borrower to ensure safety of his funds. About tangible assests we will study elsewhere in this book.

2. Liquidity. Banks are essentially intermediaries for short term funds as their deposits are largely repayble on demand or at a short notice, they lend funds for short periods and mainly for working capital purposes. The loans are, therefore, largely repayable on demand. The banker must ensure that the borrower is able to repay the loan on demand or within a short period. This depends on the nature of assets owned by the borrower and pledged to the banker. For example, goods and commodities are easily marketable while fixed assets like land, building and specialised types of plant and equipments can be liquidated after a time interval. Thus, the banker regards liquidity as important as safety of funds and grant loans on the security of assets which are easily marketable without much loss.

3. Profitability. Commercial banks are non-profit earning institutions. They must employ their funds profitably so as to earn sufficient income out of which to pay interest to depositors, salaries to staff and to meet various other estalishment expenses and distribute dividends to the share holders. The rate of interest charged by banks primarily depends upon the Bank Rate and the directives issued by the Reserve Bank of India fixing ceilings on interest rates on certain categories of advances. The variations in the rate of interest charged from different customers depend upon the degree of risk involved in lending to them. A customer with high reputation is charged a lower rate of interest as compared to an ordinary customer. The sound principle of lending is not to sacrifice safety or liquidity for the sake of higher profitability. That is to say that the banks should not grant advances to unsound parties with doubtful repaying capacity, even if they are ready to pay very high rate of interest. Such advances ultimately prove to be irrecoverable to the detriment of the interests of the bank and its depositors.

4. **The Purpose of the Loans.** While lending his funds the banker enquires from the borrower the purpose for which he seeks the loan. Banks don't grant loans for each and every purpose - they ensure the safety and liquidity of their funds by granting loans for productive purposes only, viz. for meeting working capital needs of a business enterprise. Loans are not advanced for speculative and unproductive purposes like social functions and ceremonies or for pleasure trips or for repayment of prior loan. Loans for capital expenditure for establishing businesses are of long - term nature and the banks now grant such term loans also such as buildings, plant and machinery, equipments etc. After nationalisation of banks in 1969 loans for initial expenditure to start small trade, businesses, shops, industries etc. are also given by banks i.e., goods, furniture and fixtures etc. However, commercial banks are granting loans for festivals like Diwali, Holi, Id etc. and marriage of daughter, sister to permanent employees of Government, Semi-Government, Public Sector Undertakings under schemes of consumer/ personal loans.

5. **The Principle of Diversification of Risks.** This is a cardinal principle of sound banking. A prudent banker always tries to select the borrower very carefully and takes tangible assets as security to safeguard his interests. Tangible

assests are no doubt valuable and the banker feels safe while granting advances on the security of such assests, yet some risk is always involved therein. An industry or trade may face depressionary conditions and the prices of the goods and commodities may sharply fall. Natural calamities like floods and earthquakes and political disturbances in certain parts of the country may ruin even prosperous businesses. To safeguard their interest against such unforeseen contingencies the banker follows the principle of diversification of risks based on the famous maxim 'do not keep all eggs in one basket'. It means that the banker should not lend his advances to a few big firms only or to concentrate in a few industries or in a few cities or regions of the country only. The advances, on the other hand, should be spread over a reasonable wide area distributed amongst a good number of customers belonging to different trades and industries. The banker, thus, diversifies the risk involved in lending. If a few big customers meet misfortune or certain trades or industries are affected adversely, the overall financial position of the bank will be in jeopardy.

6. National Policy and Objectives. After nationalisation in 1969, significant changes have taken place in the concept of security observed by bankers in their attitudes towards the hitherto weaker and neglected sectors of society during the last some years. The banks particularly nationalised banks have been directed to finance on a large scale to agriculturists, small industrialists, professional persons like doctors, CAs etc. and transporters etc. Security of funds lent is not sought exclusively in the tangible assets of the borrower but also in his technical competence, managerial ability, honesty and integrity etc. Loans are being given in large numbers for setting up of small businesses or for starting practice by professional persons. A Credit Guarantee Corporation has been set up to guarantee such loans. It is to be noted that bank credit has to act as an important tool for achieving wider social purpose, national policies and objectives. However, the basic principles of sound lending are funda-mental and are observed even by every prudent banker. The ways in which the basic principles are followed, of course, may be modified to suit the need of the hour.

2

Trading and Profit and Loss Account

Trading and Profit and Loss account statement is a statement of account of income and expenditure of trading/ business concern for a particular period of time on a particular date. If income is more than expenditure there is a profit and if expenditure exceeds income, there will be a loss to the business enterprise.

The information contained in trading/manufacturing account may be arranged in the following manner :

The Trading/Manufacturing Account

1. Net sales, i.e., Income by way of sale of goods or services after deducting sales returns.
2. Raw material consumed = opening stock of raw materials + net purchases during the year–closing stock of raw materials.
3. Manufacturing expenses like power and fuel, wages, stores depreciation, repairs and maintenance and other factory expenses.
4. Cost of goods sold = net sales-gross profit and hence gross profit = sales–cost of goods sold.

The Profit and Loss Account

5. Administrative and general expenses like office expenses, salaries, postage, telephone charges, licence fees, legal charges and similar other expenses.
6. Selling expenses like the salesmen's salaries and commissions, advertising and publicity.
7. Operating Profit: If the administrative, general and selling expenses are deducted out of the gross profit, it is called the operating profit. This operating profit figure if compared with the sales figure shall reveal the profit earning capacity of the business out of its operations.
8. Earning before interest and taxes (EBIT) = Operating profit + Income from other sources (i.e., receipts not connected with current operations like rent, interest, dividends earned on outside investments).
9. Profit before tax = EBIT- expenses not incidental to business like the interest on borrowings and the Investment Allowance Reserve.
10. Net profit after tax = profit before tax–taxes.

Above analysis can be put into a more direct form as under :

1. Net sales
2. Cost of sales
   (a) Raw material consumed (including stores and other items used in the process of manufacture)
   (b) Other spares
   (c) Insurance
   (d) Power and fuel
   (e) Direct labour
   (f) Repairs and maintenance
   (g) Depreciation
   (h) Other manufacturing expenses

(i) Sub Total
(j) *Add:* Opening stock-in-process
(k) Sub Total
(l) *Deduct:* closing stock-in-process
(m) Sub Total (cost of production)
(n) *Add:* Opening stock of finished goods
(o) Sub Total
(p) *Deduct:* Closing stock of finished goods
(q) Sub Total (total cost of sales or cost of goods sold)

3. Gross profit (item 1 item 2)
4. Administrative expenses
5. Selling expenses
6. General expenses
7. Interest and brokerage
8. Sub Total (4+5+6+7)
9. Operating profit (item 3 above-item 8 above)
10. *Add :* Other incomes (profit before interest)
11. *Deduct:* Other expenses (profit before tax)
12. Provision for taxes
13. Net profit after tax (item 11 above - item 12 above).

Specimen of Trading and Profit and Loss A/c of XYZ Co. Ltd. as at 31st March 2013

Particulars	*Amount* (Rs.)	*Particulars*	*Amount* (Rs.)
To Opening Stock	100000	By Sales	1300000
To Purchases	500000	By closing Stocks	200000
To Wages	50000		
To Other overheads	50000		
To Gross Profit	800000		
Total	1500000	Total	1500000
To Salaries	200000	By Gross Profit	800000
To Depreciation	230000		
To Insurance	50000		
To Intt. on bank borrowings	50000		

To General Reserve	110000		
To Capital Reserve	40000		
To Light and Water etc.	10000		
To Stationery	10000		
To Net Profit	100000		
Total	800000	Total	800000

Sd- (N.K. Jain)
Managing Director
and Chairman
Sd-(Ramjilal)
Executive Director
Sd-(V.S. Gupta)
Director (Finance)

Dated 31st May 2013
Sd- (Bhagwan Das)
Chief Accounts Officer
For R.L. Gupta and Associates
Chartered Accountants
Sd- (Ratan Lal) Partner
10, Bothra Complex, Bikaner

3

Balance Sheet Analysis

The origin of the art of modern double entry book keeping can be traced to a text by Paciolo, who was a friend of Leonardo da vinci and the text was first published in 1494. Paciolo in his treatise advised the use of several set of books for each voyage or trading journey. However, during the 14th and 15th centuries ledgers were not usually balanced at any regular fiscal periods. Only after several hundred years the present practice of yearly closing became a part of the accounting convention.

A balance sheet is a written representation of the assets and liabilities of an individual, a firm, an association, a limited company, and a corporation as on a particular date. In accounting practice Balance Sheet is divided into three parts, the assets, the liabilities and the proprietary interest, which is also termed as net worth. According to Section 210 and 211 of the Companies Act 1956, the companies have to prepare Balance Sheet at the end of each trading period in the prescribed form. However, some exemptions have also been granted under the act.

Assets are what a business organisation owns and liabilities are what it owes. In other words, liabilities shown in the Balance Sheet represent the sources of funds and assets show how these funds have been employed.

Assets and liabilities are divided into four and three groups respectively for sound analysis of financial statement.

The division is shown in the following diagram:

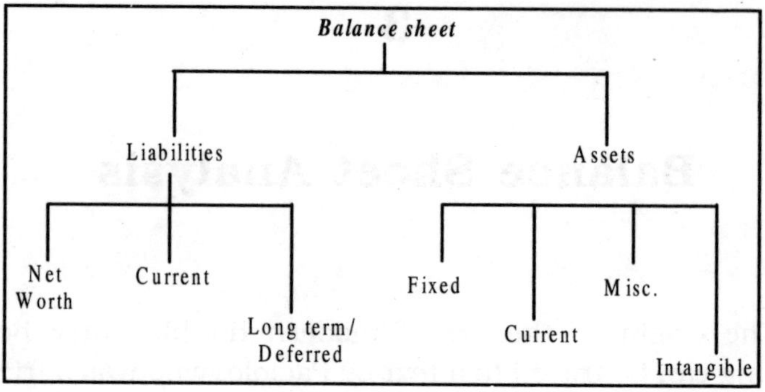

A brief description of each of these is given below:

Fixed Assets

The items of assets which are readily convertible into cash in the normal operations of a business enterprise, but which are used as an instruments of business, for production purposes, are called fixed assets.

Fixed assets represent employment of funds on a long-term basis. The following are the examples of fixed assets:

(a) Land
(b) Building
(c) Machinery, tool, equipments
(d) Truck, car
(e) Furniture and fixtures.

In a small concern all the items do not appear in the Balance Sheet whereas in the Balance Sheet of a large company all the items may constitute fixed assets. The value at which these items will be quoted in the Balance Sheet may be the original cost less depreciation. It may also be a figure based on revaluation.

A fixed asset accounting plays an important role. Depreciation is nothing but a deferred amortization of the cost of fixed assets on notional rate of wear and tear of the assets. Every asset has a limited time span of usefulness and, therefore, a decremental value should be accounted. Generally, two methods of calculation of depreciation are in use in India.

(1) Straight method

(2) Diminishing balance method

Under the first method a fixed amount is written off every year while under the second method depreciation is provided at a fixed percentage of the outstanding net block each year. Depreciation is a notional charge on the profit beneficial to the enterprise as it reduces tax liability.

Current Assets

Current assets are such assets which move within a period of 12 months in ordinary course of business through various processes of production, distribution and payment of goods, until they become cash or its equivalent, by which debts may be readily and immediately paid. Current assets represent employment of money on a short-term basis. Following are the examples of current assets:

(a) Cash in hand or cash in bank.

(b) Marketable securities.

(c) Raw materials, stock-in-process, finished goods.

(d) Accounts receivables (book-debts/sundry debtors).

Miscellaneous Assets

There are certain visible items in the assets, which are not converted into cash in the normal course of business and they are not used as an instrument for the running of the day-to-day operations of the business. These assets, which are tangible in nature called miscellaneous assets. A few examples are given below:

(a) Investments in non-marketable securities.
(b) Non-consumable spare parts and stores.
(c) Advances to directors and employees.
(d) Other loans and advances.
(e) Prepaid expenses (relating to future expenses beyond one year).

Intangible Assets

These assets are not available for payment of debts of a going concern and depreciate greatly in the event of liquidation of the concern. Rarely they appear in the balance sheet of a small concern. A few such items are:

(a) Patents
(b) Copyright
(c) Trademark
(d) Formulas
(e) Preliminary and formation expenses.
(f) Loss incurred by the concern.

A company or business enterprise may be of two types:

Private Limited Company

In a private limited company the capital is provided by the shareholders. The shareholders are the owners of the private limited company. Shareholders cannot transfer his share without the consent of other shareholders of private limited company.

Public Limited Company

In a public limited company the shares are easily transferable and capital is provided by the owners, promoters and the public. Capital in company represents money provided by the owners, promoters and the public.

Capital of a company or business enterprise is of four types namely:

1. Authorised Capital

The capital, a company is legally permitted to issue, is called the authorised capital.

2. Issued Capital

Part of the capital for which subscription is invited is called issued capital.

3. Subscribed Capital

Part of the capital agreed to be taken up by shareholders is subscribed capital.

4. Paid-up Capital

The amount actually paid by shareholders towards capital is called paid-up capital.

Classes of Shares

Broadly speaking, there are two types of shares. Ordinary shares and preference shares. Variations in the rights which these give exist to meet different requirements.

1. Ordinary Shares. Ordinary shares normally form the backbone of the capital structure. Although they may be issued at a premium or at a discount they do have a fixed nominal value, which is not changed unless there is a special reason. The ordinary share capital is usually termed "Equity Capital."

Ordinary share-holders are entitled to share of the surplus profits after the debenture-holders and preference share-holders have received their fixed rate of interest or dividend. Sometimes the view is put forward that whole of the profits, after payment to preference dividends, should go to ordinary share holders, but this appears to be a purely theoretical concept and is not borne out by actual practice. The necessity to appropriate profits to reserves means that the surplus available to ordinary share-holders in depleted. It is, therefore, very clear that because of the risk involved in having to take second place to the preference share-holders a company will normally pay a higher rate of dividend than that in respect of the preference shares otherwise it would have great difficulty in attracting necessary amount of capital. Any attempt to obtain finance by the issue of ordinary shares should show that future expectations are quite attractive. The attractive rate of earnings should be at least that obtainable elsewhere on capital which carries similar risks.

Ordinary shares usually carry with them a right to vote at company meetings. Since the ordinary shareholders bear a heavy responsibility it seems only fair that they should have the power to vote. Non-voting ordinary shares also exist. Deferred or founders' shares are a type of ordinary share often of small nominal value, which entitle the holders - possibly company promoters or vendors of the business to surplus profits after the other ordinary shares have received a certain fixed amount.

2. Preference Shares. As the name "Preference Shares" implies, the holders have prior claims, before ordinary share-holders, to dividends and possibly, in the event of liquidation, to repayment of capital. The rights do not extend to the preference share-holders being given privileges before debenture holders or other lenders. The latter's are creditors, and therefore must be satisfied before there is any thought of payment of dividends.

Preference shares generally carry a right to a fixed rate of dividend and are described to show this fact on the company's Balance Sheet or other statements. This right may be carried forward from year to year, if a dividend is not paid in one year, then the right to it is carried forward to the next and subsequent years. These are "Cumulative Preference Shares". On the other hand, if failure to declare a dividend in a particular year cancels the right to that year's dividends, then the shares are said to be "Non-Cumulative". Sometimes preference shareholders are given the right to a second dividend, when the shares are called "Participating." They may also be entitled to be paid back a part of capital upon liquidation.

The right for the company to redeem may also be a feature of a preference share issue. Certainly this is something which must not be overlooked when preparing a capital structure. If the rate of dividend required to attract funds is particularly high, then a company may find that redeemable preference shares would be beneficial. When interest and therefore dividend rates fall a company may be able to redeem the old preference shares from the proceeds of a new issue made on more advantageous terms. Shares can be redeemed only if the Articles so provide. Moreover, they should be fully paid up and they must be replaced either by a new issue of shares or if redeemed out of profits, there must be an equivalent amount transferred to the Capital Redemption Reserve Fund.

A conversion privilege may be used as an attraction for investors. At some time in the future the preference shareholders may be given a right to convert the shares held into ordinary shares from the company's stand point it should be noted that the existence of this right is sometimes viewed as being an indication of lack of financial strength. The company, it is argued, is unable to obtain funds without offering some extra inducement. There may be some truth in this statement.

Care has to be exercised when fixing the price at which the conversion privilege can be exercised. There should be a gap between the present value of ordinary shares and the price which must be reached before the conversion can be made.

Loan Capital-Debentures

A debenture is a document by which a company acknowledges a loan. The terms for repayment, the interest payable and the charge, if any, on company's assets, will be stipulated.

Debentures do not form part of the share capital, but are generally referred to as "Loan Capital". Debenture holders are not share-holders. If the debentures provides for a charge on company assets, then the debenture holder is a creditor with special privileges. When there is no charge conferred then the lender is an ordinary, unsecured creditor.

There are different classes of debentures. The naked debenture is a bare promise to repay the loan and, until the loan is repaid, it states the interest payable.

Debentures may confer a floating or a fixed charge on a company's assets. The floating charge does not attach to any specific asset, and therefore may allow the company to change to meet changing conditions. A floating charge may crystallize when a company goes into liquidation when a receiver is appointed, or when one of the conditions stated on the debentures occurs. From the management point of view the preservation of control without possible interference from mortgage debenture holders is clearly an advantage. The borrower, on the other hand, may not find the floating debenture as attractive as the mortgage debenture. The former allows a company to create mortgage debentures which rank in priority next to the existing floating debentures.

When a fixed charge is given on company's assets the debentures are generally called "Mortgaged Debentures".

Debentures may be issued to named persons and registered by the company, or they may be made payable to bearer. In the latter case the debentures are negotiable instruments, so that they can be transferred with ease from one person to another. In addition to registration by the company it is necessary for any charge created by a company to be registered with the Registrar of Companies within 21 days.

Debentures may be issued in perpetuity; alternatively, they may be issued as being redeemable at some future date.

There is no doubt that the issue of debentures provides a convenient method of obtaining finance. If made at appropriate time, when interest rates are not high, money may be obtained at reasonable cost. Interest payable to debenture holders is a charge against profits and is paid direct to the Commissioners of Inland Revenue, only the net amount being paid to debenture holders.

Discount and Premiums

Shares are often issued at a discount at a figures less than nominal value or at a premium at a figure in excess of nominal value. Debentures may be issued at a discount. Say, a Rs. 1000 debenture for Rs. 990.

The newly formed company can't issue shares at a discount, because by law the issue at a discount must be of a class of shares already issued and must be in respect of a company which has been entitled to carry on business for at least one year. Permission of the court must also have been given.

A company is free to issue debentures at a discount at any time, because they do not form part of share capital.

No special legal requirements are needed for the issue of shere at a premium. The guiding factor should be the market value of the existing shares which carry similar rights to the proposed new issue. Expected future earnings will also influence the premium which may be charged.

If the new issue is likely to water the capital to the extent that the percentage earnings on capital employed will be reduced, then this fact should be brought into the valuation, and, therefore the price asked for each new share.

Reserves

Reserves of a company or business enterprise always represent the amount, which is readily available to the company for spending.

Reserves are of two kinds—capital and revenue reserves. Capital reserve is created out the profit that is not made from the normal operations whereas revenue reserve is created out of profit made in course of company's normal operations.

Capital reserve arises in the following cases:

(1) Surplus due to revaluation of fixed assets.
(2) Issue of shares at a premium.
(3) Profits from sale of fixed assets and investments.
(4) Redemption of shares/debentures/bonds at a discount.
(5) Capital subsidy by the Government.

Generally capital reserves are not available for distribution, except in case of item no. 3 above when it is received in cash, they are perpetual reserves, revenue reserves represents the profit from the operations after meeting all the expenses and retained in the business. In other words, the revenue reserves are past profits, which are not drawn by the shareholders as dividends. Some examples are:

1. General reserve
2. Development rebate reserve
3. Investment allowance reserve
4. Capital debenture redemption reserve.

On the above item 2, 3 and 4 are specific reserves and cannot be utilized by the company for declaring dividends.

For instance, both development rebate and investment allowance reserves are tax rebates or concession allowed to the company to induce it to go in for acquisition for further capital equipments. It must be that reserves whether capital or revenue, belong to the shareholders. Net worth theoretically reflects the surplus that might remain at the time of company's liquidation after paying all other liabilities from sale proceeds of all the assets of the company if net worth accounts for 35 per cent of the total assets it would mean that in case of liquidation on an average every asset has to realise at least 65 paisa of each rupee invested in it, so that the creditors and lenders are paid. The surplus of net worth over the paid-up capital reflects the policy of plough-back of profits followed by the management.

Networth

Net worth is the amount of funds invested at the risk of business. In other words, it is liability of the business organization to those interested in it after all the debts of every description have been paid. It is the sum of the following items appearing in the Balance Sheet:

1. Proprietor's capital or paid-up share capital.
2. Reserves
3. Undistributed profits.
4. Retained earnings.

Current Liabilities

These are short - term liabilities which are encountered in the normal course of business and which are due and payable within a year. Current liabilities generally consist of one or several of the following items:

1. Short - term borrowings including bills discounted
2. Deposits maturing within a year
3. Sundry creditors
4. Interest and other charges accrued but not due for payments

5. Provision for taxation
6. Instalments of term loans/debentures/deferred payments credits due within a year.

Term Liabilities

Liabilities which are payable after a period of one year from the date of Balance Sheet are classified as term liabilities. Therefore, term liabilities are long - term liabilities of the organisation.

Following are some examples:

1. Debentures, Fixed deposits (not maturing within a year).
2. Term loans (exclusive of instalments payable within a year).
3. Deferred payment credits (exclusive of instalments payable within a year).

Contingent Liabilities

There are certain items in respect of which the company may not be in a position to ascertain the correct picture at the time of preparation of the Balance Sheet. These obligations, which may or may not arise on future date are called contingent liabilities. A few examples are:

1. Pending suit laws.
2. Claims against the company not acknowledged as debt.
3. Guarantees issued by the company.
4. Unexpired portion of the L/Cs established by banks.
5. Taxes and duties under dispute with Authorities.
6. Bills and cheques discounted by banks.

Specimen of Balance Sheet of XYZ Co. Ltd., Bikaner as on 31st March 2013, Head Office 5 Industrial Area, Rani Bazar, Bikaner is shown below:

Liabilities	*Amount] (Rs.)*	*Assets*	*Amount (Rs.)*
Share capital:		Goodwill at cost	50,000
(a) Authorized capital:		Fixed assets:	
100000 ordinary shares of Rs. 10 each = Rs. 10,00,000		(a) Property at cost (land and buildings)	8,00,000
(b) Issued and paid-up capital:		(b) Plant and machinery at cost Rs. 3,00,000 Less Dep. 1,80,000	1,20,000
75000 ordinary shares of Rs. 10 each fully paid	7,50,000	Furniture & fixtures	20,000
Bank borrowings	3,00,000	Motor car at cost Rs. 2,50,000 *Less* Dep. 50,000	2,00,000
Capital reserve	40,000		
General reserve	1,10,000	Current assets:	
Profit and Loss a/c balance i.e. net profit	1,00,000	(a) Stock in trade	2,00,000
Statutory liability, if any:		(b) Sundry debtors	80,000
Future tax liability	50,000	(c) Cash at bank	20,000
Current liabilities		(d) Cash in hand	5,000
(a) Sundry creditors	50,000		
(b) Taxation	20,000		
(c) Proposed dividend	75,000	1,45,000	
Total	14,95,000	Total	14,95,000

Sd/-
(N.K. Jain)
Managing Director
Sd/-
(Ram Ji Lal)
Executive Director
Sd/-
(V.S. Gupta)
Director (Finance)

Sd/-
(Bhagwandass)
Chief Accounts Officer

For R.L. Gupta & Associates
Chartered Accountants
Sd/- (Ratanlal) Partner
10, Bothra Complex, Bikaner.

However, following important points should be taken care of and noted while studying financial statements viz. Balance Sheet and Profit and Loss Account from bankers point of view:

Sales Turnover

This is the first important point, which should be observed in financial statements. Sales turnover of the unit is compared to that in the previous years to ascertain whether there is satisfactory increase in the same, over the years. This by itself is not enough to ensure sound health of the unit, because, there can be increase in sales turnover despite a decline in the volume of sales due to inflationary tendencies. However, stagnation or decline in sales should be taken as a warning bell by the bankers, unless there are satisfactory reasons, corrective steps should be taken to reverse the trend.

Capital Base

The capital base includes the paid-up capital and reserves less the losses, if any. The capital the stake of the owners and it bears a relationship to the activities and turnover of a unit. It can be compared with sales turnover to find out how many times the capital is rotated. It varies from industry to industry depending upon the cash accruals. In case the turnover is abnormally high, it can be construed that the unit is over-trading, which again, is not good for a unit.

Sundry Debtors Vs Sales Turnover

A comparison is to be made between these two figures. In case cash accruals matches the level of traders then the overtrading can be over-looked. But, if market credit provided by the unit is relatively high, it can land the unit into financial stringency.

Debt-Equity Ratio

Much is talked about this ratio in banking circles. A higher debt equity ratio is an eye opener as it reveals the extent to which the unit is dependent upon the market borrowings apart from bank/ financial institutions. It can be possible that banks funds may in due course be diverted to meet the market obligation or current assets may be liquidated for the purpose, resulting in reduction in the value of securities.

Working Capital Margin

One of the principles of good financial management is that a part of the long-term resources represented by capital and reserves be utilised/ available for acquisition of current assets. Therefore, the working capital margin (capital and reserves less losses, if any) minus fixed assets or current assets minus current liabilities should come out of this. So if there is reverse trend, i.e., the unit tries to utilise short - term resources to acquire long - term assets, it is inviting trouble and banker should take it very seriously.

Inventory

A look at the inventory build up can reveal whether the party is speculating by building up a stock of raw materials abnormally then the requirements, in the belief that prices will go up in future. This will result in maximum utilisation of bank limits blocking some essential payments, which may result in unpleasantness and ultimately lead to misutilisation of scarce bank funds.

Also a large build up to finished goods or trading goods may reveal that market demand is declining which is resulting into stagnation of stock causing unit to become sick. Similarly raw material consumption can be compared with closing stocks and finished goods with sales turnover to get useful clues.

Profitability

An enterprise must generate enough surpluses to service its borrowing and capital. A comparison of profitability over the past few years (say at least 3 years) are made to ensure that the percentage of gross profit and net profit in relation to sales turn over is at least constant, if it has not improved.

A larger turn over is of no use if there is not proportionate increase in the profits.

Bank Accounts

To quote a few cases the conduct of an account is another major issue, which no banker can ignore. If sales bills drawn by party are not realised within a reasonable period or these are returned of and on, it can be construed that something worse is in the offing and immediately the banker should take corrective steps.

Similar, inference can be drawn in case of cheques sent in clearing or outstation cheques purchased by banker, when these are returned. The review of accounts reveals many interesting feature. Credit summations in the accounts can be directly compared with sales turn over. It indicates that the party is maintaining accounts somewhere else through which it passes major part of its sales proceeds. Similarly, excess turnover on credit side indicates market borrowing or dealings of an accommodation nature or other firms enjoying pipeline funds in clearing.

Again, when account remains fully drawn or over-drawn for a long time and the party is unable to meet its commitments despite adequate limits the banker should try to find the reasons, which may reveal that funds are somewhere blocked. It could be undesirable investments, market lending, build up of inventory or debtors for goods or investments into acquiring fixed assets. The causes should be investigated and banker should take precautionary steps.

Stock Statement

Timely submission of statement of inventory is of utmost importance. It gives the security available to the bank, reveals slow moving of stocks, old stocks and value of the stocks. All these should be carefully examined and compared with past trends to arrive at conclusions.

Visits

Periodical visits to the establishment of the borrower for verification of securities and seeing the working of the unit afford a golden chance for detecting warning signals, if any, it is possible to detect:

1. Shortage/difference in actual stockholding and one revealed in stock statements and books.
2. Slow movement of finished goods and accumulation of raw material.
3. Excess valuation of stock with reference to purchase bills.
4. Manipulation of stocks.
5. Inclusion of unpaid for stocks.

Importance of Balance Sheet

The Balance Sheet is a summary of firms assets and liabilities, including share capital and reserves at a defined moment of time. It is, therefore, said as a snapshot or still, picture of the financial position of a business entity. It is also called the mirror of the actual financial position of a business enterprise.

In addition to Profit and Loss A/c, the various groups interested in the company can also draw useful inferences from an analysis of the information contained in the Balance Sheet, share holders usually have twin interests: an interest in receiving a regular income and an interest in the appreciation of the investment in shares. The market worth of their shares depend not only on dividends they receive but also on the extent of retained earnings built up by the company. Investment decisions of the prospective investors and disinvestment decision of the existing investors (share holders/ Debenture holders/ bond holders) are influence by the composition of assets and liabilities shown in the Balance Sheet.

The Balance Sheet reflects the financial position of the enterprise. It provides useful information to various users of information i.e. creditors, investors, share-holders, debenture holders, bond-holders and Government and its agencies etc who might be interested in the business enterprise. A proper analysis of the information contained in the Balance Sheet can enable them to draw conclusions which in turn help them in taking decisions.

Similarly, other interested parties like regulatory and development agencies of the Government, consumer and welfare organizations can derive useful information and get conclusions from the study of the Balance Sheet about the working of the corporate sector and its contribution to the national economy.

4

Cash and Fund Flow Statement-Concept and Utility

It is very important for a banker to gauge the health of borrowal unit and also to assess the need-based credit requirements of his client. The tools which a prudent banker should adopt includes Ratio Analysis, Funds Flow Study, Break Even Analysis, Sensitivity Analysis etc. Although the above tools are effective and do serve the purpose to great extent, they suffer from certain infirmities for, e.g., all the approaches are on accrual basis or in other words adopt a funds flow approach.

Cash and Fund Flow Statement

Cash Flow statement is a statement of receipts of cash and payments of cash for a given period. The cash flows of an enterprise receipts and payments are analysed under certain specific heads to cater to the requirements of the users. Information about the cash flow of an enterprise is useful in providing the users of financial statements with a basis to assess the ability of the enterprise to generate cash and the needs of an enterprise to utilise the cash. Cash budget is summary statement containing forcasted figures of receipts and payments of cash over a given period of time which is usually 12 monthly basis.

Terminology used in Cash Flow Statements are

Cash. Comprises cash on hand and demand deposits with banks.

Cash equivalents. Cash equivalents are short-term highly liquid investments that are readily convertible into known accounts of cash and which are subject to insignificant risk of changes in value.

Cash Flows. Cash Flows are inflows and outflows of cash and cash equivalents.

Operating activities. Operating activities are the principal revenue producing activities of the enterprise and other activities that are not investing or financing activities.

Investing activities. Investing activities are the acquisition and disposal of long-term assests and other investments not included in cash equivalents.

Financing activities. Financing activities are activities that result in changes in the size and composition of the owner's capital (including preference shares capital in the case of a company) and borrowings of the company.

Operating activity. Operating activities are the principal revenue-producing activities of the enterprise. Therefore, they generally result from the transactions and other events that determine the operating profit or loss. The amount of cash flows arising from the operating activities is key indicator of the extent to which the operations of the enterprise have generated sufficient cash flows to maintain the operating capability of the enterprise, pay dividends, repay loans and makes new investments without recourse to external sources of financing. Examples of cash flow from operating activities are as under:

(a) Cash receipts from the sale of goods and the rendering of services.

(b) Cash receipts from royalties, fees, commissions, interests, rents and other revenues.

(c) Advances received from customers.

(d) Cash payments to and on behalf of employee.

Investment Activity

Investment activities represent cash flows to the extent to which expenditures have been made for resources intended to generate future income and cash flows. Examples of cash flows arising from investing activities are:

(a) Cash payments to acquire fixed assets.

(b) Cash receipts from disposal of fixed assets.

(c) Cash payments to acquire shares, warrents or debt instruments of other enterprises and interests in joint ventures (other than payment for those instruments considered to be cash equivalent of those held for dealing or trading purposes.)

(d) Cash receipts from disposal of shares, warrants of debts instruments of other enterprises and interest in joint ventures (other than payments for those instruments considered to be cash equivalents or trading purposes).

(e) Cash advances and loans made to other parties (other than advances and loans made by a financial enterprise).

Financing Activities

The separate disclosure of cash flows arising from financing activities is important because it is useful in predicting claims on future cash flows by providers of funds (both capital and borrowings) to the enterprise.

Examples of cash flow arising from financing activities are:

(a) Cash proceeds from issuing shares and other similar instruments;

(b) Cash proceeds from issuing debentures, loan, notes, bonds and other long - term and short term (other than bank overdraft) borrowings.

(c) Cash repayments of amounts borrowed, and
(d) Dividend paid.

Once we are familiar with classification of inflows and the outflows of cash, we can plot the flow on a monthwise basis under respective categories viz., Operating, Investing and financing activity. This would enable us to draw up a summary of the cash flows on a monthly basis as under:

(I) Operating balance of cash/cash-equivalent for the month.

(II) Add/Less: Net Increase/decrease in cash/cash equivalents represents aggregate position of net cash from:

(a) Operating activity (b) Investing activity (c) Financing activity.

(III) Deficit/surplus of cash/cash equivalent for the month {(I) + or (-) (II)}

When we have drawn up the summary of cash flow for each month we will be in a position to determine the exact cash requirement or cash surplus for that particular month as the case may be. The enterprise can accordingly plan the steps to be taken to fund this deficit by resorting to short-term bank borrowings or plan for deployment of surplus, if any.

Cash Flow and its Utility for Bankers

In the credit policy of April 1995, RBI had introduced the loan system of delivery of Bank credit and the present guidelines are that for borrowers with FBWC limit of Rs. 10 crores and above the loan component would be minimum of 80 per cent. In credit policy declared by the RBI in April 1997, RBI has given freedom for banks to evolve their own methods of assessing working capital requirements of borrowers within prudential guidelines and exposure norms. As a sequel to the instructions all banks had formulated their lending policy which inter alia provides for an option to the borrower with FBWC limit of above 10 Crores rupees to have their working capital credit requirement assessed based on cash budget.

Note. FBWC represents fund based working capital.

Performa Showing Cash Flow Statement

Sources of Funds	*Amt. (Rs.)*	*Uses or Application of Funds*	*Amt. (Rs.)*
Operations		Dividends	—
Net Profit after Taxes		Non-operating Losses not	
Add Depreciation		Passed through P & L a/c	—
other Amortisations		Redemption of Redeem-	
Funds Provided by		able Preference Share	
Operations	—	Capital	—
New Issue of		Repayment of Deb/Bonds	—
Share Capital	—	Repayment of Long-terms	
New Issue of		Loans	—
Debentures/Bonds	—	Purchase of Fixed Assets	
Additional Long-term		Purchase of Long-term	—
Borrowing from Bank/		Investments	—
Financial Institutions	—	Increase in Balance of	
Sale Proceeds of		Working Capital	—
Fixed Assets	—	(Current Assets-Current	
Sale of Long-term	—	Liabilities)	
Investments	—		
Total	—	Total	—

Fund Flow Statement

An analysis of the fluctuations of current assets and current liabilities, i.e., working capital tells us how the working capital has increased or decreased. We want to know where the increased working capital is applied if it has increased, and from where funds have been released if it has decreased. The P & L A/c gives some indication of the results of operations and its impact on the funds position. We try to integrate the impact of operations reported in the P & L A/c and Balance Sheet by preparing a statement of changes in financial position. It describes the sources from which funds were received and uses to which funds were put. This statement of changes in financial position is usually referred to as fund flow statement or statement of sources and application of funds.

As its name tells us that fund flow statement traces the flow funds through the organisation. In other words, it shows the sources from where the funds were raised and the uses to which they were put.

The statement of funds flow is usually bifurcated into two logical divisions sources of funds or inflows during the periods and uses of funds or applications of funds during the period. The division showing sources of funds summarises all those transactions which had the net effect of increasing the working capital. Uses of funds on the other hand deal with all those transaction which had the effect of decreasing the working capital. We shall illustrate the primary structure of flows as under:

The flow of funds statement gives us a summary of impacts of managerial decisions. As such it reflects the policies of financing, investment, acquisition and retirement of fixed assets, distribution of profits, and the success of operations.

Importance of Cash and Fund Flow Statements

Cash is another form of fund though in narrow sense, it refers to supply that can be drawn upon according to need. Here the term includes both cash and cash equivalents. Cash equivalents are highly liquid short-term investments which could be easily converted into cash without much delay.

It may, however, be appreciated that the obligations and liabilities arising on a day to day basis must be met through "Cash" or "Cheque". We must also be able to distinguish between "Profit" and "Cash". One cannot pay the creditors, electricity bills, taxes or even dividend by "Net Profit". For such and many other purposes, a business enterprise needs either physical cash or balance or credit limits with banks. Not to be able to meet the business commitments through cash as and when these arise can spelt disaster for a business even if it has a strong working capital and has earned handsome profit.

IN FLOWS

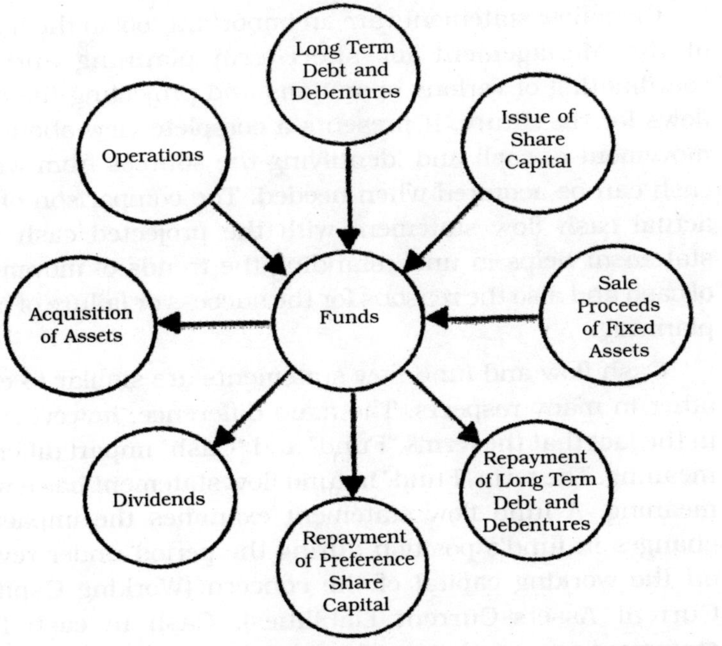

OUT FLOWS

(Chart Showing Basic Flow of Fund)

So far we have seen that the Balance Sheet and P & L A/c provide us information about the financial position and results of operations in a financial period. The funds flow statement explained earlier traces the flow of funds through the organisation. But neither of these financial statements can provide information about the cash flows relating to operating, financing and investing activities.

To ensure that the right quantity of cash is available in accordance with the needs of a business, it is necessary to make a "Cash Planning" by determining the amount of cash entering the business (Cash inflows) and the cash leaving the business (Cash outflows). The statement which explains the changes that take place in cash position between two periods is called the cash flow statement.

Cash flow statements are an important tool in the hands of the Management for short-term planning and co-coordinating of various operations and projecting the cash flows for the future. It presents a complete view about the movement of cash and identifying the sources from which cash can be acquired when needed. The comparison of the actual cash flow statement with the projected cash flow statement helps in understanding the trends of movement of cash and also the reasons for the success or failure of cash planning.

Cash flow and fund flow statements are similar to each other in many respects. The main difference, however, lies in the fact that the terms "Fund" and "Cash" impart different meaning. The term "Fund" in fund flow statement has a wide meaning. A fund flow statement examines the impact of changes in fund's position during the period under review on the working capital of the concern (Working Capital= Current Assets–Current Liabilities). Cash in cash flow statement refers only to cash and or balance with bank i.e., a small part of the total fund, although very important. The cash flow statement starts with the opening cash balance, shows the sources from where additional cash was received and also the uses to which cash was put and ends up showing the closing balance as at the end of the year or period under review. Whereas there are no Opening and Closing balances in fund flow statement. Increase in current assets or decrease in current liabilities increases working capital, whereas the decrease in current assets or increase in current liabilities increases the cash flow or decreases working capital.

Example

M/s Laxmi Udyog 10, Rani Bazar Industrial Area, Bikaner (Rajasthan)

Balance Sheet as at	*31st March 2012 Amount (Rs.)*	*31st March 2013 Amount (Rs.)*
Assets:		
Freehold Property	150000	150000
Plant and Machineries *less* Depreciation	110000	170000
Goodwill	15000	5000
Investment	75000	130000
Debtors	108000	130000
Stock	70000	104000
Bills Receivables	42000	53000
Cash-in-hand and at Bank	20000	50000
Preliminary Exp.	20000	15000
Total	**610000**	**807000**
Liabilities:		
Share Capital		
(40000 Equity Shares @ Rs. 10/-Each)	400000	500000
Share Premium	—	60000
General Reserve	50000	65000
Dividend Equalization Reserve	25000	15000
P & L A/c	40000	55000
Sundry Creditors	60000	67000
Provision for Taxation	20000	35000
Bills Payable	15000	10000
Total	**610000**	**807000**

Additional Information

1. Shares were issued at premium of Rs. 1.5 per share.
2. During the year taxation liability in respect of_____ was Rs. 20,000 and paid.
3. During the year Rs. 10,000 was provided for depreciation on plant and machinery.
4. An item of the plant the written down value Rs. 20,000 was sold at Rs. 25,000.

5. During the year a dividend @ 7.5 per cent was paid.
6. Part of the investment costing Rs. 30,000 was sold at Rs. 35,000 and the profit was taken in Profit and Loss Account.

For arriving at the figures necessary for preparation of cash flow statement, we have to prepare Investment Account, Plant and Machinery Account, Provision for Taxation Account and Adjusted or Revised Profit and Loss Account.

Investment Account

Particulars	*Amt. (Rs.)*	*Particulars*	*Amt. (Rs.)*
To Opening Balance	75000	By Sale	35000
To P & L A/c (profit on sale)		By Closing Balance	130000
25000–20000	5000		
To Bank (130000–75000			
= 55000+30000)	85000		
Total	165000	Total	165000

Plant and Machinery Account

Particulars	*Amt. (Rs.)*	*Particulars*	*Amt. (Rs.)*
To Opening Balance	110000	By Sale	25000
To P & L A/c (profit on sale)			
25000–20000	5000	By depreciation	11000
To Bank (170000–110000	91000	By Closing Balance	170000
= 60000+20000+11000			
= 91000)			
Total	206000	Total	206000

Provision for Taxation Account

Particulars	*Amt. (Rs.)*	*Particulars*	*Amt. (Rs.)*
To Bank	20000	By Opening Balance	20000
To Closing Balance	35000	By P & L A/c	35000
Total	55000	Total	55000

Adjusted P and L Account

Particulars	*Amt. (Rs.)*	*Particulars*	*Amt. (Rs.)*
To General Reserve (65000–50000)	15000	By Opening Balance	40000
To Dividend (400000×7.5%)	30000	By Dividend Equalisation Reserve (25000–15000)	10000
To Provision for Taxation	35000	By Plant and Machinery. Profit on Sale	5000
To depreciation	11000	By Investment–Profit on Sale	5000
To Goodwill (15000-5000)	10000	By Profit for the Year or	
To Preliminary Expenses (20000–15000)	5000	Closing Balance as on 31.3.2013 (balancing figure)	101000
To Closing Balance	55000		
Total	161000	Total	161000

Statement of Cash Flow for the Period 1.04.12 to 31.03.13

Particulars				*Amt. (Rs.)*
To Opening Cash Balance as of 31.03.12				20000
Add/ (deduct) cash flow from operating activities				
Net Profit (P & L adj. a/c)			101000	
Add:				
Decrease in Current Assets				
Sundry Creditors (67000-60000)=		7000	7000	
Deduct:			108000	
Increase in Current Assets				
Debtors (132000–108000)	24000			
stock (104000–70000)	34000			
Bills Receivables (53000–42000)	11000	69000		
Decrease in Current Liabilities:				
Bills Payable (15000-10000)	5000			
Payment of Tax	20000	25000	94000	+14000
Add/ (deduct) cash flow from Investment activities:				
Add: Sale of Plant and Machinery	25000			
Add: Sale of Investment	35000	60000		
Deduct: Purchase of Plant and Mach.	91000			
Deduct: Purchase of Investment	85000	176000		-116000
Add/ (deduct): Cash flow from				

Financing activities		
Add: Issue of Share Capital	100000	
Share Premium	60000	
	160000	
Deduct: Payment of Dividend	30000	+130000
Closing Cash Balance as on 31.03.13		48000

Assessment of Working Capital Based on Cash Budget

Hitherto Banks were assessing the working capital limits of sugar/tea industry and construction companies based on cash budgets. Recent RBI guidlines also provide for assessing the working capital requirement of Software and Information Technology Industry by adopting cash flow approach. As detailed above the lending policy of some of banks extend this facility to other borrowers also.

The quantum of bank finance can be assessed by identifying the maximum deficit as projected in the Cash Budget. The maximum deficit would be fixed as the limit. Let us assume that the net monthly deficit/suplus for a unit is as under:-

(Rs. Crores)

Month	Jan	Feb	Mar	April	May	June	July	Aug.	Sep.	Oct.	Nov.	Dec.
Monthly surplus/ deficit	-100	-200	-150	-300	-400	-550	-700	+500	+450	+800	+900	+1000

In the above example the limit would be Rs. 700 crores. However, monthly/quarterly drawings would be regulated based on projected monthly/quarterly deficit for the ensuing month/quarter.

Assessment of working capital based on cash flow is also best suited for consideration of sanction of adhoc limit/one time transactions, etc., of seasonal units, i.e., cotton gining, sugar industries etc. Cash budget is a handy tool to assess the working capital requirement of seasonal business with irregular cash flows during a financial period.

Based on the projected Balance Sheet and cash flows bankers would be in a position to decide the quantum of loan, the timing and the repayment schedule within the overall limit. Cash-flow statements are also of use for determining the unit's ability to meet maturing obligations like Letter of Credit/Letter of Guarantee liability.

Monitoring of Advances

In order to have an effective control over borrowal units the banker must be able to fairly gauge how much money a customer needs for how long it would be needed and how funds will be obtained for repayment. The cash budget or cash forecast can answer these questions quite precisely. Based on information/data so obtained the account can be effectively monitored.

The cash budgeting approach is particularly useful for monitoring borrowal units who have been granted working capital limits in the form of loan.

The annual cash budget is to be supplemented with monthly or quarterly cash budget to enable the banker to ensure that the unit is proceeding as per plan on healthy lines. In case any deviations are observed based on monthly cash budgets corrective measures can be initiated immediately before the problem assumes unmanageable proportions.

Further, Cash Budgets will also enable the banker to get a precise idea about the long term cash requirements of the borrower and whether the same is proposed to be funded appropriately.

In the end, a cash flow statement when used in conjunction with the other existing tools like ratio analysis, funds flow statement, etc., would help a banker to have a better understanding of the need of the borrower thereby enabling him to manage the account more effectively and efficiently. A study of the monthly cash-budgets would forewarn a banker of mis-matches which have either been committed or contemplated. "To be forewarned is to be forearmed."

5

Ratio Analysis

For a lending agencies like banks, the Balance Sheet of a company forms one of the basic and critical documents while taking a credit decision, be it for working capital or project finance. The Balance Sheet and Proft and Loss Account statements of an enterprise gives a treasure of information if properly analysed. These statements which reflect the financial soundness and operating efficiency of a corporate greatly facilitates the lending agencies to arrive at a credit decision.

The Balance Sheet of an enterprise is a snap shot indicating the financial health of an enterprise on a particular date and does not throw any light on the current state of affairs as mostly the time difference between the close of the books of accounts and its discloser will be relatively too long baring a few exceptions. Further, the Balance Sheet has certain limitations and does not disclose some of the following critical factors.

Critical Factors

(A) Managerial competence

(B) Technical experience

(C) Turnover of people

(D) Obsolescence of technology

(E) Competition and

(F) Marketing

It is desirable that in the appraisal memorandum in addition to commenting on the financial parameters of the corporate, the above off the balance sheet information should be detailed in order to make the appraisal exercises more meaningful. The Profit and Loss Statements of the corporate which discloses the sales, production, profitability, performance and the cash flows during the accounting period will be of more relevance to the lending agencies to determine the operating efficiency of the corporate in managing its resources for maximisation of returns.

A ratio can be worked out between two variables having either cause and effect relations or connected with each other in some other manner. These two variables can be selected either from Balance Sheet or from P & L A/c or one from Balance Sheet and another from P & L A/c.

The lending agencies normally rely more on the following ratios while assessing the working capital and the project finance to a corporate borrower:

(A) Current Ratio

This ratio indicate the solvency of the company to meet the liabilities, which are due for payment with in next 12 months from out of current assets. This ratio is calculated based on the current assets and current liabilities as on the last day of the accounting year and it is quite possible that this can be easily managed even on the last date of the Balance Sheet by any corporate. Though the lending agencies derive a lot of comfort from this ratio, in reality the ratio may not reflect the true picture about the solvency of the company as the realisable value of the current assets in the event of forced sale cannot be determined as against the current liability which are clearly quantified. It is not uncommon that even many going concerns having comfortable current ratio will be struggling to meet the day to day commitments due to improper cash management. Likewise, a corporate not having comfortable current ratio will be meeting all its maturing obligations without much delay due to efficient cash management.

As the assessment of working capital requirement is done based on projected Balance Sheet keeping the audited Balance Sheet as a base, it is desirable for lending agencies to relate this ratio with other operating ratios which give qualitative analysis on cash management efficiency of the corporate.

$$\text{Current Ratio} = \frac{\text{Current Assets}}{\text{Current Liabilities}} = \frac{305000}{145000} = 2.1:1$$

Ideal Ratio = 1.33:1

(B) Total Outside Liabilities to Net Tangible Worth

This ratio is calculated by dividing the total liabilities of the company with the tangible net worth of the company. This ratio reflects the financial soundness and the solvency of the corporate. Lower the ratio indicate the high degree of solvency and higher the ratio indicates the over extended financial position of the company. Normally bankers feel comfortable as long as this ratio does not go beyond 3:1 for any corporate.

Ideal Ratio: 2:1 for medium and large units.
3:1 for SSI units

(C) Debt (Long - term) Equity Ratio

This ratio is calculated by dividing the long-term loans with tangible net worth of the company. The ratio signifies the financial soundness of the corporate. Lower the ratio indicates the high solvency and higher the ratio indicates high debt gearing of the corporate. Mostly, the term lending institutions use this ratio as a yardstick for the purpose of appraisal of the term loan requirements of the corporate.

Ideal ratio is 2:1, which lending institutions normally accept for project finance.

(D) Debt (Long - term) Service Coverage Ratio

This ratio is calculated by dividing the cash accruals with the term loan obligations, which falls due during the accounting period. This ratio will enable the term lending institutions to evaluate the viability of the proposal and determine the period of the term loan and also to fix up a suitable repayment shedule depending on cash accruals during the tenor of the term loan.

Ideal Ratio is 1:1.5, which is normally considered desirable by the term lending institutions.

Other suggested ratios are:

(1) *Capacity utilisation/installed capacity Ratio*

This ratio will indicate the following:

1. Extent of capacity utilisation.

2. Whether the growth in sales is on account of increase in production or in selling price per unit of production of increase in production or increase in production and decrease in selling price per unit of production etc. It is possible that the company can always maintain the growth in sales not by increase in the volume of production but mere increase in selling price per unit of production also.

3. Reasons for decrease/stagnation in the production in terms of quantity can be ascertained like fall in demand, introduction of new substitutes in the market by its competitors, production bottlenecks, labour problems, new technology etc.

4. Future capacity expansion can always be subjected to a closer scrutiny in the event of any increase in the fixed assets being reflected in the CMA.

(2) *Net Block/long term debt Ratio*

In most of the working capital advances, there is a practice of stipulating second charge on fixed assets of the company where the same are charged to term lending institutions. The above ratio will indicate the asset coverage ratio for the term lenders which in turn will indicate the cushion available for working capital bankers also being the second charge holders. Further, this ratio will also highlight the investment made in the fixed assets for expansion/ diversification and redemption/rescheduling of long - term debts depending on the increase/decrease in the ratio on an ongoing basis.

(3) *Inventory and receivables/total current assets ratio*

This ratio will indicate the extent of funds that are deployed in the form of production linked assets like inventory and receivables. Notwithstanding the fact that the corporate has brought in the required margin on the total current assets as per the assessment made in the CMA, the bankers always regulate the drawings in the cash credit account based on the fully stocks declared on the stock-statement less margin to arrive at the drawing power. Normally, there should be proper match in building up the production linked assets to the other curret assets depending on the specific requirement of the corporate normally, the carry of inventory is influenced by the level of activity/availability of raw material and the receivables depending on the trade practices/ supply and demand. At the same time any unreasonable level of carry of inventory and receivables are not desirable, as it would unnecessarily block the working capital resulting in cash flow problems. In any given situation, it is always comfortable for the working capital bankers if the ratios indicates sufficient cushion for the drawings in the working capital limits as otherwise the working capital limits will throw irregularity for want of adequate level of inventory and receivables. Further, no yard-stick can be fixed for carry of inventory and receivables and the other current assets which would be normally based on the past trend and depending on the various other factors like production cycle, availability of raw materials, transit-time for procurement of the new-materials, the trade practices with regard to availability of credit in the composition of current assets (whether inventory and receivables on the current assets) should attract closer scrutiny by the bankers.

(4) *Other current assets/total current assets Ratio*

This ratio will indicate the percentage of other current assets to the total current assets. This ratio can be used to determine the extent of working capital funds deployed for building up the other current assets. As other current assets do not directly support the economic activity of the company as such any abnormal variation in the ratio can be subjected to various interpretations.

(5) *Ratio of deployment of long-term funds to long - term and short - term uses*

The following ratios will indicate the pattern of application of the long-term funds to various uses (both long term and short term). By using these ratios, the working capital bankers can wherever possible prevail upon the corporate from deploying the long-term funds for certain long term uses in the event of any short fall in the minimum net working capital to be brought in by the corporate is noticed.

(a) Repayment of term liabilities/total sources of funds:

This ratio will indicate the extent of long - term sources used for repayment of dues under long - term loans.

(b) Dividend payments/long - term sources:

This ratio will indicate the percentage of outflow of long-term funds by way of dividend to the share-holders.

(c) Increase in fixed assets/total long - term funds:

This ratio will indicate the percentage of long - term funds used for acquisition of fixed assets.

(d) Other long - term uses (increase in intangibles, loss, other non-current assets)/total long - term funds:

This ratio will indicate the percentage of long-term use.

(e) Long - term suplus (or deficit)/long-term sources:

This ratio will indicate the percentage of the long - term funds available for net working capital as margin from the corporate.

(6) *Raw materials consumed/closing stock of raw materials*

This ratio will compare the extent of raw materials holding as closing stock with reference to the raw-materials consumed during the accounting period (year). This ratio can be used to analyse whether the corporate has purchased the raw-materials much in excess of annual requirement. The ratio will indicate how many times the raw material have been turned over during the accounting period. Higher the ratio, there will be a healthy turn over of raw materials and faster movement of working capital cycle. Lower the ratio, there will be slower movement of working capital cycle and slow movement of the inventory. Further, this will also indicate whether the company has been carrying over a period of time if the trend continues.

(7) *Total assets (net of intangible)/Net worth*

This ratio will indicate the extent to which owned funds are invested in building up the assets of the corporate. A low ratio indicates the lesser dependence on the outside borrowings and plough back of cash accruals into the system. A high ratio will indicate the increased dependence on the outside borrowings to run business. This will indicate the prudence of the management in conserving the internal cash generation for building up the assets of the company.

(8) *Cost of production/net sales*

This ratio will indicate the operating efficiency of the corporate and the increasing ratio will indicate the inability of the corporate to pass on the rising cost of inputs to the end users of the product. This will indicate the falling/rising profits margin of a corporate, which will put the lenders on guard while making further financial commitments to the corporate.

(9) *Other expenses (selling, general and administrative etc.)/net sales*

This ratio can be used to find out whether the non operating expenses of the company is increasing/decreasing in proportion to the growth in the sales. These expenses are more or less in the nature of fixed expenses, the ratio will be on a declining trend with the increasing sales and will be increasing with the decreasing sales. This ratio can be used to determine the ability of the corporate to meet the other expenses out of its operations.

(10) *Interest/total borrowings (including sundry creditors)*

This ratio will indicate the average cost of funds borrowed by the company to run it's business. This will enable the lender to determine the rate at which the corporate is borrowing from outside sources. High ratio indicates the desperate attempt of the borrower to manage its funds requirement by resorting to high cost borrowings, which will have direct impact on bottom-line of the corporate.

(11) *Raw Material Consumed/cost of production Ratio*

This ratio will indicate the cost of raw materials consumed in relation to the cost of production. The increasing ratio will indicate the inability of the corporate to pass on the additional cost to the end users of the product. This ratio can also be used to know whether there is any high percentage of rejection/wastage of raw-materials on account of outdated technology employed by the corporate, change in Government policy of foreign trade etc.

(12) *Net sales/total working capital employed (total current assets or total current liabilities/net working capital)*

This ratio will indicate the number of times the company has been able to turnover the total working capital employed by the company. Normally if the ratio settles between 4 and 8, it can be inferred that there is a healthy turnover in the working capital. If the ratio goes beyond 8, there is possibility of the corporate indulging in over trading.

(13) *Net sales to bank-borrowings*

This ratio will indicate whether the increase in the bank borrowing is proportionate to the increase in the sales or not. If the corporate is not able to reach the level of a activity as envisaged at the time of appraisal of the working capital limits and avails the limits assessed to the full extent or beyond the limits assessed, it should put the lenders on guard about the possible diversion of funds. This ratio can be used to ascertain the cause of such action and refrain the corporate from indulging in such diversions.

(14) *Interest/operating profit before interest*

This ratio will indicate the ability of the corporate to service the interest on the loan taken from the lenders. If the ratio is decreasing, it gives an indication that corporate is generating sufficient profits to service the interest on the loans borrowed. It will increase the comfort level of the lenders in taking higher explosure to the corporate. If the ratio is increasing, the bottomline of the corporate gets affected due to additional out-flow of cash to meet the increasing interest costs.

(15) *Other income/net profit (before taxes)*

This ratio will indicate the extent of not-operating income contributing to the total profit of the company. A low ratio will indicate that the net profit is being generated more from the operations. A high ratio should put the lenders on guard as it will give wrong signals that income from operations is coming down over a period of time and the corporate may run into losses from the manufacturing activity as not-operating income cannot become a regular source of income to any corporate.

(16) *Net profit/sales*

This ratio will indicate the profitability of the corporate in relation to the volume of the sales achieved. Even though the profit of the corporate in absolute terms may be increasing but in terms of the percentage to sales it may be shrinking. This ratio will reflect whether the corporate is able to maintain the profitability in relation to the growth in sales. Otherwise, it gives a clear indication that the profit margin is on the decline and the corporate is not in a position to pass on the increased input costs.

(17) *Net Sales/receivables*

This ratio can be used to determine the number of times the receivables have been turned over into cash. A high ratio indicates the ability of the corporate to sell the product and realise its receivables faster. A low ratio signifies the poor demand for the products and the inability of the corporate to collect the receivables.

(18) *Net sales/inventory*

This ratio can be used to determine the number of times the inventory has been turned over in the accounting period. A high ratio indicates a good turnover of inventory. If the ratio is low, it indicates that the corporate may be carrying slow moving stocks.

Conclusion

Analysis of a Balance Sheet of a corporate is one of the very effective exercises, if properly carried out can give a treasure of information on the efficiency of the corporate in managing its business, to the lenders (Bankers), while taking short - term or long - term investment decisions. The Balance Sheet and the operating statement are interrelated and the information available are very much required to be properly blended and leveraged into financial ratios for technical analysis. The suggested additional ratios are supplemental to the existing ratios which are being used by the lenders in order to make the credit appraisal exercise more effective and meaningful in the backdrop of the mounting Non-performing Assets (NPA) with the lenders and accountability factor hanging on credit analysis like a democles sword.

Other Important Ratios

1. Liquidity or Acid Test Ratio

$$\text{Formula} = \frac{\text{Quick Assets (Current Assets–inventory and prepaid expenses)}}{\text{Current Liabilities}}$$

This ratio tells us the company's capacity to pay off claims of current creditors immediately, i.e. liquidity of the concern.

Net Working Capital= Current assets – Current Liabilities

= Rs. 305000—Rs. 145000

= Rs. 160000

2. Working capital/Turnover Ratios

(i) *Net Sales*

Working capital (current assets–current liabilities)

This ratio tell us the extent to which existing resources are being utilised for achieving a certain level of turnover.

(ii) $\frac{\text{Stock (Inventory)}}{\text{Working capital}} = \frac{\text{Rs. 200000}}{\text{Rs. 160000}} = 1.25:1$

(iii) $\frac{\text{Book debts or (Accounts Receivables)}}{\text{Working capital}} = \frac{\text{Rs. 80000}}{\text{Rs. 160000}} = 0.5:1$

3. Profitability Ratios

(i) Gross profit Ratio = $\frac{\text{Gross profit} \times 100}{\text{Net sales}} = \frac{\text{Rs. 800000}}{\text{Rs. 1300000}} \times 100 = 61.54\%$

(ii) Net profit ratio = $\frac{\text{Net profit before or after tax} \times 100}{\text{sales}} = \frac{\text{Rs. 100000}}{\text{Rs. 1300000}} \times 100$

$= 7.69\%$

(iii) Operating profit ratio = $\frac{\text{Operating profit} \times 100}{\text{Sales}} = \frac{\text{Rs. 250000}}{\text{Rs. 1300000}} \times 100$

$= 19.23\%$

(operating profit = net profit +capital reserve+General reserve = Rs. 100000+Rs.40000+Rs. 110000=Rs. 250000)

4. Activity Ratios

(i) Stock (Inventory) turnover ratio = $\frac{\text{Sales}}{\text{Average Stocks}} = \frac{\text{Rs. } 1300000}{\text{Rs. } 150000} = 8.67 \text{ Times}$

(ii) Debtor's Turnover = $\frac{\text{Annual Credit sales}}{\text{Average Debtors}} = \frac{\text{Rs. } 80000}{\text{Rs. } 30000} = 2.67 \text{ Times}$

(iii) Fixed Assets Turnover = $\frac{\text{Sales}}{\text{Fixed Assets}} = \frac{\text{Rs. } 1300000}{\text{Rs. } 1140000} = 1.14:1$

Precautions

(1) Only the figures which have mutual cause and effect relationship should be considered. The ratio of sales to fixed assets is useful one for it tells us the output (in terms of sales) obtained from the investment of one rupee in fixed assets; the ratio of sales to the nominal capital is quite meaningless for there is no relationship between the two.

(2) Ratios for different years should be tabulated in a tabular form. The changes in ratios then become significant.

Ratios are expressed in mathematical terms, like percentage or the number of times or in numbers. Some ratios are better expressed when worked out in percentage like the gross or operating profits to sales. But certain ratios appear to be more effective when expressed in the number of times like stocks turnover. Two interdependent items like the current assets and current liabilities or debt and equity can be better compared, if expressed in numbers like 3:1 and 2:1.

(3) The particular characteristics of the industry should always be kept in mind while a firm is being studied. For instance, if any industry is seasonal, ratios at a particular point of time will always differ from ratios at the end of the year or throughout the year—the particular point of time of study, therefore, becomes important.

(4) Last, but not the least, it should be remembered that the main objective of a firm/company should be to earn satisfactory profit and not to be able to display acceptable ratios. In other words, a management should be able to take decisions which would yield good results but which may throw some ratios out of reasonable proportion temporarily. Some concerns, towards the close of the year, deliberately start bringing down stocks of materials in order to show a good (rather low) inventory ratio (in relation to sales or total sales) and then spend money unnecessarily to build up stocks as otherwise production would be hindered.

Limitations of Ratios

Ratios, like statistics, have an air of precision and finality about them which at times may be misleading. It is, therefore, important to know some of the drawbacks from which they suffer:

1. Ratios generally portray the relationship between two items in statement of account. But the relationship can be interpreted only after studying the reality behind the statements. For example, an increase in stocks, in relation to sales, may be a good sign, provided it is the result of an anticipated rise in demand, but it would be otherwise if there has been a recession in trade. On this account, it is usually difficult to interpret a ratio by mere reference to the statement from which it has been constructed.

2. A ratio being an arithmetical statement of relationship between two variables, can be accurately interpreted only if the effect of change in prices, which may have taken place, if adjusted in values of both the variables. For example, while computing the ratio of sales fixed assets are revalued at their replacement cost, it would give a brighter picture than that justified by the circumstances.

3. Ratios are as accurate as the accounts on the basis of which these are established. Therefore, unless the accounts

are adjusted accurately by applying correct values to assets and liabilities the statements prepared therefrom would not be correct and the relationship established on that basis would not be realistic.

6

Break-Even Analysis

Break-even analysis is also helpful for bankers to assess the financial strength of the concern. Basically it is concerned with finding of the point at which revenues and cost agree exactly - hence the term 'Break-Even'. The break-even point is, therefore, the volume of output at which neither a profit nor a loss is incurred. Formula is as under-

$$\text{Break-Even Point} = \frac{F}{1-(V/P)}$$

where

F - Fixed costs

1 - A whole number (One)

V - Variable cost per unit (or total variable cost)

P - Selling price per unit (or total sales value)

Example: Supposing that in a soap factory, figures of a week are as under:

(a) Fixed cost for the year is Rs. 50,000

(b) Variable cost per unit for the single product being made is Rs. 3

(c) Estimated sales for the period i.e. week is valued at Rs. 1,20,000

(d) Each unit sells at Rs. 15 each

$$\text{Break-Even Point} = \frac{F}{1-(V/P)}$$

$$= 50000/\{1-(3/15)\}$$

$$\text{Break-Even Point} = 50000 / (4/5)$$

$$= \text{Rs. } 62{,}500$$

It is, therefore, apparent that Break-Even Point is a position of a manufacturing concern at which the concern does not earn any profit. After this stage the concern starts earning profit, which is shown in the chart given below.

Break Even Chart

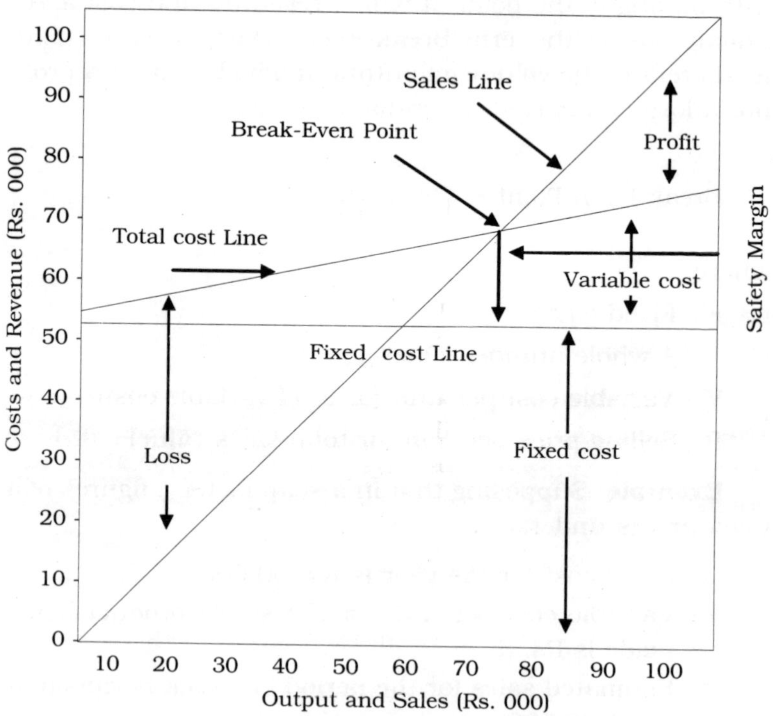

Output and Sales (Rs. 000)

7

Depreciation

Business organisation are required to record the purchase of long-lasting, substantial property and equipment (such as computer, vans, furniture, buildings etc.) as assets in the financial records, and to charge a portion of the cost of these items to each year in which they have a useful life. This process is known as capitalizing and depreciating fixed assets.

Depreciation is the allocation of the cost of an asset over a period of accounting and tax purposes.

It can also be defined as a decline in the value of a property due to general wear and tear or obsolescence, opposite of appreciation.

For example, suppose on 1st January an organisation acquires a computer with an estimated useful life of four years. The computer costs Rs. 2500. On recording the purchase, the following entry in the Journal is made :

Fixed Asset (increase by) Dr. 2500.

To Cash (decrease by) Cr. Rs. 2500

(Being purchase of a computer for Rs. 2500)

At the end of each of the next four fiscal years, including the current year, the Journal entry will be made. Depreciation expense (increases by) Rs. 2500/4 = Rs. 625 Dr. per year.

To Accumulated depreciation (increases by) Rs. 625

(Depreciation expense for the year)

It is very important to remember that the cash for the computer was spent in the first year. However, one - fourth of the expense for the computer will appear in the statement of activity (Income Statement or Profit and Loss A/c) for each of the four years, that it is deemed to have a useful life. Therefore, in three years after the purchase, a depreciation expense of Rs. 625 will appear in the financial statements even though no cash was spent during those years.

Accumulated depreciation, as the name implies, reports on the amount of depreciation, which has accumulated over time. By the end of first year, one-forth of the computer will be depreciated. At the end of second year, two-fourth (i.e. one half) will be depreciated. By the end of the fourth year, the computer will be fully depreciated. In other words, the full cost of computer will have been recorded as an expense.

The fixed asset portion of the statement of position (Balance Sheet) will represent this accumulated depreciation for the computer as given below :

Year-1

Computer (cost)	Rs. 2500
Less Accumulated Depreciation	Rs. 625
Net fixed assets	Rs. 1875

Year-2

Computer (cost)	Rs. 2500
Less Accumulated Depreciation (625+625)	Rs. 1250
Net fixed assets	Rs. 1250

Over the remaining two years, accumulated depreciation will increase by Rs. 625 per year and net fixed assets will decrease by Rs. 625, until the accumulated depreciation is Rs. 2500 and net fixed assets is zero.

In this example, the organisation determined that the useful life of the computer was four years, and that after the end of that time the computer would have no remaining value. Most non - profit making organisations charge an equal amount of depreciation expense to each year of an asset's useful life. This is called straight line depreciation.

To calculate the depreciation charge for each fixed asset, we must know how much the asset costs (including all costs necessary to make the asset operational), how long the asset can reasonably be expected to last before it needs to be replaced, and whether it will have any salvage value at the end of its useful life. Since there are certain conventions for items such as computers, vehicles, furniture, buildings and other fixed assets, we should consult our accountant or expert in accounting matters i.e. Chartered Accountant etc. when estimating the useful life of a new capital purchase.

Since depreciation expense is a non-cash expense (i.e. cash is usually paid out in the year the asset is acquired/ purchased, but the expense is distributed over several years), it is important to plan for the replacement of fixed assets as they wear out or become obsolete. For example, some organisations set aside an amount of cash equal to the amount of their yearly depreciation expense so that money will be available to purchase a new asset once the current one is fully depreciated.

Straight-Line Method

This method of calculating depreciation of an asset, which assumes that the asset will lose an equal amount of value each year. The annual depreciation is calculated by subtracting the salvage or remaining value of the asset from the purchase price, and then dividing this number by estimated useful life of the asset. This method assumes a constant depreciation value per year. This method spreads the total depreciation cost evenly over the asset's useful life.

Assuming that:

The price of a depreciating asset as P and its salvage value after N years as S,

Annual depreciation

$$= \frac{(\text{Cost} - \text{Residual value})}{\text{estimated useful life}} = (P - S)/N$$

If P = Rs. 20000, S = Rs. 5000 and N = 5, the annual depreciation would be [(Rs. 20000–Rs. 5000)/5] = Rs. 3000

Diminishing or declining balance method. This is a rapid depreciation method in which the percentage rate is applied to the residual balance rather than to the original cost. Recall that the straight line method assumes a constant depreciation value. Conversely, the declining balance method assumes a constant depreciation rate per year. Also, like the sum of years method, more depreciation tends to occur earlier in the asset's life.

Let us assume the price of a depreciating asset is P and its salvage value after N year is S. We could assume the assets depreciates by a factor of (or a rate of %).

This method is known as single declining balance method. In an equation, this looks like :

Annual depreciation = Previous year's value × percentage rate

Therefore, for our illustration the depreciation during the first year is (Rs. 20000/5) = Rs. 4000. Following table describes how the declining balance would depreciate the asset:

Year	*Depreciation*	*Year-end Value (Rs.)*
1.	(Rs. 20000/5) = Rs. 4000	16000
2.	(Rs. 16000/5) = Rs. 3200	12800
3.	(Rs. 12800/5) = Rs. 2560	10240
4.	(Rs. 10240/5) = Rs. 2048	8192
5.	(Rs. 8192/5) = Rs. 1638.40	6553.60

Salvage Value (S) = Rs. 6553.60

There are several methods of depreciation which differ from one another only from the stand-point of how the cost is treated as expiring over the life of the asset. We have discussed only two most commonly used methods. The following ideas must be clear while dealing with depreciation:

(a) ***Original cost of the assets*** : This is the cost incurred in making the asset available for use in the first instance.

(b) ***Salvage Value*** : The expected recovery or sales value of the asset at the end of useful life.

(c) ***Useful life*** : The expected time period for which the asset is to provide economic service i.e. the period for which the asset could be used for production/ service.

(d) ***Depreciable cost*** : This is original cost less salvage value. This is the amount of expense the enterprise will be incurring on account of expired costs of the machine over its useful or economic life.

(e) ***Written down value*** : Written down value of an asset at any point of time is original cost less depreciation to date (accumulated depreciation). This is also referred to as book value.

8

Bank Reconciliation Statement

In a business, the majority of payments are made through banks where huge payments are involved, it is very risky to carry that much amount of cash. Therefore, a businessman or trader will carry a cheque book with him that enables him to make any payment from Rs. 1 to Rs. 1 Crore or even more by simply drawing a cheque.

In the cash book of a trader, a bank column is provided on both sides. Bank account is personal account. When, a cheque is received and deposited in the bank, the trader debits his bank account by applying the principle of personal account, debit the receiver. When a cheque is issued for payment of any expense or for the purchase of goods/ services, bank will make payment, on presentation of the cheque, provided there is sufficient balance to pay/honour it. The trader records the entry on the credit side of the cash book applying the principle: credit the giver. The trader records these entries immediately.

In a bank, the customers account is opened, based on the same principle, banker credits the customer's account when a cheque deposited by a trader, is cleared and debits his account, when a cheque, drawn by him, is presented to it for payment.

In this chapter, we shall examine the causes for differences in the balance in the cash book, maintained by the trader, and the pass-books maintained by the bank, as also the process of reconciling balances.

Need for Bank Reconciliation

The trader records the deposits and withdrawals in the cash book immediately. The bank, however, records these on the dates of clearing of the cheques and on the dates when the cheques are presented for payment over the counter or through the process of a clearing house. Thus, the dates of entries in the cash book and pass book may differ and balances shown by cash book and pass book may not tally.

For example, a trader receives a cheque for Rs. 100000 from his customer on 31st May and deposits it into his bank account on the same date.

The bank will credit the same to his account only after clearance of the same from the bank on which cheque is drawn. This process may take about three to four days or even more, if the cheque is an out-station cheque. Under the circumstances, a trader can not issue any cheque to his supplier or anyone else until the amount is credited in his bank account. It is, therefore, necessary to reconcile the balance shown as per the cash book and the balance as per the pass book. The statement that is prepared for reconciling these two balances, together with explanations is called the 'Bank Reconciliation Statement', which is normally prepared at the end of each month by the trader.

Causes of Differences

The main causes that lead to disagreement in balance of the cash book and the pass book are as follows:

(1) ***Cheques issued but not presented for payment*** **:** A trader immediately records the payment by a cheque to a creditor or, for any expense, in the cash book credit side (payment side). The debit for the same, however, will appear in the pass-book only when payee presents the cheque for payment to the bank. There is usually a time lag between the date of issue of the cheque by the drawer and presentation by the payee.

(2) ***Cheques deposited into bank but not yet collected:*** In a business, majority of receipts will be by cheques. The customers will issue cheques to the trader on the bank where they have an account, say, Punjab National Bank, Dena Bank, Syndicate Bank, Central Bank of India, State Bank of India and so on. As and when the cheques are received, he will deposit these in his bank account and entries will be immediately recorded in the cash book on the debit side (receipts side). His banker, however, will credit the amounts of the cheques, to the customers account, on the dates of clearance of cheques by the clearing house. There is a time lag between the date of deposit of the cheques in the bank by the trader and that of credit in his account in the bank.

These two entries (1) and (2) will appear first in the cash book and then later on in the pass book.

Now, there are certain entries that originate in the pass book first and then from the pass book, the trader makes the necessary entries in the cash book.

(3) ***Bank Charges*** **:** For collection of outstation cheques, payments made as per standing instructions, issue of cheque books, issue of duplicate passbook or statement of account etc. the bank will debit customer's account.

(4) ***Interest on Savings Bank Account*** **:** The bank credits the customer's account in the pass book for the interest on the credit balance.

(5) ***Interest on overdraft*** **:** When a trader draws more than what he has in the bank account, the account is said to be over-drawn. This facility is normally

availed by a trader with prior arrangements/limits with his bank. The banker debits the customer's account for the interest on an overdrawn balance.

(6) ***Amount collected by Bank on Standing Instruction*** : The trader often issues some standing instructions, authorising his banker to collect on his behalf certain amounts due to him, such as interest, dividend etc. On receipt of an advice from the bank, the trader records the same on the debit side of the cash book.

(7) ***Amount paid by Bank on Standing Instruction*** : The trader may instruct the banker to pay a certain amount on a particular date on his behalf, e.g. life Insurance premium, locker rent, light and water bills, reservation of air/train tickets etc. Entries for the same transactions will be recorded in the cash book of the trader on the credit side on the receipt of the bank advice or after comparing pass book with the cash book.

(8) ***Direct payments into the bank made by trader's customers*** : Many a time, customers directly, deposit amounts into the trader's bank account. After clearing these cheques, the banker will credit these amounts to the trader's account. Entries for the same transactions will be recorded in the cash book of the trader on the debit side, on receipt of the bank advice or after comparing the pass book with the cash book.

(9) ***Dishonour of a cheque*** : On dishonour of a cheque deposited by the trader, the bank will debit the customer's account.

(10) ***Errors*** : While recording the entries, the banker or an accountant might make some errors such as under-casting, over-casting, recording entry in cash or discount column, crediting the amount in some other account and so on. Due to these errors, bank balance and cash book balance may not tally.

Illustration

The bank column of a cash book showed a debit balance of Rs. 29000 on 30.06.2013. Prepare a bank reconciliation statement as on 30th June 2013 and show the balance as per pass book on the basis of following causes of difference:

1. Cheques sent to bank for collection but not collected upto 30.06.13 Shyam Sunder Rs. 9000 and Mohan Rs. 15000.
2. Ram Lal deposited Rs. 10000 directly in the bank account of the trader.
3. Bank allowed Rs. 100 as interest.
4. Cheque issued to Shyam Lal for Rs. 15000 but not presented for payment.
5. Bank paid directly LIC premium Rs. 5000.
6. Bank charges were Rs. 50, not yet entered in the cash book.

Answer:

Bank Reconciliation Statement as on 30th June 2013 (Cash Balance Method)

Particulars	*Amount (Rs)*	*Amount (Rs)*
Balance as per cash book		29000
Add (+) (i) Ram Lal directly deposited in the Bank	10000	
(ii) Interest allowed by Bank	100	
(iii) Cheque issued but not presented	15000	25100
		54100
Less (-) (i) Cheques deposited into bank		
Shyam Sunder 9000		
Mohan 15000	24000	
(ii) LIC Premium paid by bank	5000	
(iii) Bank charges	50	29050
Balance as per bank pass book (Cr)		25050

Remember that:

(a) When there is a positive balance, it appears as a debit balance in the cash book and a credit balance in the bank pass book.

(b) When there is over-drawn balance, it appears as a debit balance in the bank pass book but as credit balance in the cash book.

Illustration 2

Prepare bank reconciliation statement as on 31st Dec. 2012 from the following details and show the balance as per bank pass book.

(i) Credit balance as per bank column of cash book Rs. 40000 (over-draft)

(ii) Cheques issued but not presented for payment Rs. 10000.

(iii) Cheques deposited into bank but not yet collected Rs. 15000.

(iv) Bank charges Rs. 200 not entered in cash book.

(v) Interest on investment collected by bank was not entered into the cash book Rs. 3000.

(vi) Water bills paid directly by bank Rs. 1000.

Answer:

Bank Reconciliation Statement as on 31st December, 2012 (Cash Balance Method)

Particulars	*Amount (Rs)*	*Amount (Rs)*
Balance as per cash book (Cr or over-draft)		40000
Add (+) (i) Cheques deposited into bank but not yet collected	15000	
(ii) Bank charges not yet entered in cash book	200	
(iii) Water bills directly paid by bank	1000	16200
		56200
Less (i) Cheques issued but not yet presented for payment	10000	
(ii) Interest on investments collected by bank but not entered in cash book	3000	13000
Balance as per bank pass book (Debit or over-draft)		43200

Alternatively, we can prepare Bank reconciliation statement showing (±) signs in the following manner:

Bank Reconciliation Statement as on 31st December, 2012 (Cash Balance Method)

Particulars	Amount (Rs)	Amount (Rs)
Balance as per cash book (Cr or over-draft)		(–) 40000
Add (+) (i) Cheques issued but not presented for payment	10000	
(ii) Interest on investments collected by bank but not yet entered in cash book	3000	(+) 13000
		(–) 27000
Less (i) Cheques deposited into bank but not yet collected	15000	
(ii) Bank charges not yet entered in cash book	200	
(iii) Water bills directly paid by bank	1000	(–) 16200
Balance as per Bank pass book (Debit or over-draft)		(–) 43200

This method is easy to understand for students as there is no change if the balance is positive (Debit) as per cash book except to remember signs (±)

Now, we shall see how the Bank Reconciliation Statement is prepared if balance as per bank pass book is given (Credit and over-draft/debit)

Illustration 3

From the following particulars, prepare a bank reconciliation statement as on 31.03.2013

(i) Debit balance as per bank pass book (over-draft) Rs. 15000

(ii) Charged interest on over draft. Rs. 500

(iii) Cheques for Rs. 15000 were deposited into bank in March but a cheque of Rs. 2500 was collected in April 2013.

(iv) Cheques issued in March for Rs. 25000 out of which cheques for Rs. 5000 were paid in May 2013.

(v) A customer deposited Rs. 2500 directly in bank account.

(vi) Bank paid municipal tax under standing instructions Rs. 1000.

Bank Reconciliation Statement as on 31.03.2013 (Pass Book Balance Method)

Particulars	*Amount (Rs)*	*Amount (Rs)*
Balance as per bank pass book (Dr or overdraft)		15000
Add (i) Cheques issued but not presented for payment	5000	
(ii) Customer directly deposited into bank	2500	7500
		22500
Less (i) Cheques sent for collection but not yet collected	2500	
(ii) Interest on over-draft charged by bank	500	
(iii) Payment directly made by bank: municipal tax	1000	4000
Balance as per cash book (Credit or overdraft)		18500

Alternate method

Bank Reconciliation Statement as on 31.03.2013 (Pass Book Balance Method)

Particulars	*Amount (Rs)*	*Amount (Rs)*
Balance as per pass book (Debit)		(–) 15000
Add (i) Cheques sent for collection but not collected	2500	
(ii) Interest charged on overdraft	500	
(iii) Payments directly made by bank: municipal tax	1000	(+) 4000
		(–) 11000
Less (i) Cheques issued but not yet presented for payment	5000	
(ii) Customers directly deposited into bank account	2500	(–) 7500
Balance as per cash book (Credit or overdraft)		(–) 18500

Illustration 4

Prepare Bank Reconciliation Statement as on 30th June 2013 from the following informations:

(i) Credit balance of bank pass book was Rs. 10800.

(ii) Cheques sent for collection into bank Rs. 10000 out of which cheques for Rs. 1200 were not collected.

(iii) Cheques issued but not yet presented for payment of Rs. 1500.

(iv) Interest allowed by bank on deposits Rs. 350.

(v) Bank charged as incidental expenses Rs. 25

Answer:

Bank Reconciliation Statement as on 30.06.2013 (Pass Book balance method)

Particulars	*Amount (Rs)*	*Amount (Rs)*
Balance as per pass book (Credit)		10800
Add (i) cheques sent for collection but not yet collected by bank	1200	
(ii) bank charged as incidental expenses	25	1225
		12025
Less (i) cheques issued but not presented for payment	1500	
(ii) interest allowed by bank on deposits	350	1850
Balance as per cash book (debit)		10175

How to prepare a Bank Reconciliation Statement when extracts of Cash Book and Pass Book are Given?

When the cash book and pass book abstracts are given, the following points should be noted :

(i) Find out the period for which both the abstracts are given.

(ii) Compare the cash book debit side with the pass book credit side and the cash book credit side with the pass book debit side.

(iii) When the period for which both the abstracts are given is common i.e. the cash book abstract relates to January and the pass book abstract is also given for January, take into account only uncommon entries.

(iv) When the period for which both the abstracts are given is uncommon the cash book relates to January but the pass book relates the February, take into account only common entries.

(v) Where period is same, uncommon entries will appear in the reconciliation statements.

(vi) When the period is different, common entries will appear in the reconciliation statement.

Illustration 5

From the following extracts of the cash book (bank column only) and the bank pass book of Suresh Trading Co., prepare a bank reconciliation statement, as on 31st Dec. 2012.

Cash Book

Dr. Cr

Dec. 2012	*Particulars*	*Amount (Rs.)*	*Dec. 2012*	*Particulars*	*Amount (Rs.)*
1	To Balance b/d	12500	4	By Goyal,	3000
10	To Mamta	3000	8	By Pitre	4000
15	To Geeta	5000	10	By George	2000
20	To Vidya	8000	15	By Joshi	8000
29	To Sheela	10500	25	By Black	5000
30	To Dividend	840	30	By White	100
				By Madan Lal	4000
				By Balance c/f	13740
		39840			39840

Bank Pass Book

Dec. 2012	Particulars	Withdrawals (Rs.)	Deposit (Rs.)	Balance (Rs.)
1	By Balance b/f		12500	Cr. 12500
6	To Goyal	3000		Cr. 9500
10	By Mamta		3000	Cr. 12500
	To Pitre	4000		Cr. 8500
16	By Geeta		5000	Cr. 13500
18	To Joshi	8000		Cr. 5500
22	By Vidya		8000	Cr. 13500
25	By Dividend		480	Cr. 13980
28	To Black	5000		Cr. 8980
31	To LIC Premium	500		Cr. 8480
	To Balance C/f	8480		
		28980	28980	

Answer

Bank Reconciliation Statement as on 31st Dec. 2012

Particulars	Amount (Rs.)	Amount (Rs.)
Balance as per Cash Book (Debit)		13740
Add (i) Cheques issued but not presented		
George	2000	
White	100	
Madan Lal	4000	6100
		19840
Less Cheques deposited but not collected as yet		10500
Dividend amount recorded more in cash book (840–480)		360
LIC Premium paid but not recorded in cash book	500	11360
Balance as per pass book		8480

Adjusting the Cash Book Balance

We have seen that certain entries appear in the pass book first and then by comparing the pass book with the cash book, these missing entries are incorporated in the cash book, the trader must know the correct bank balance at any time so that he can issue cheques only to the extent of the available bank balance. Therefore, before preparing a bank reconciliation statement, the accountant/AO makes the necessary correction in the cash book and adjust the cash book balance.

The items, which can usually be adjusted in the cash book are as follows :

(i) Payment made by bank as per standing instructions.
(ii) Bank charges, interest on overdraft debited by the bank.
(iii) Collection of interest on securities and dividend on shares by bank.
(iv) Debits for the dishonour of cheques in the pass book.
(v) Direct deposits made by customers of the trader.
(vi) Errors committed in the cash book.

Advantages of Bank Reconciliation Statement

The advantages of preparing bank reconciliation statement are as under:

(1) It helps the management to check the accuracy of the entries made in the cash book.
(2) It helps to detect errors and to take timely action for correction of balances.
(3) It is very important control technique for the management.
(4) It shows the correct bank balance at any particular time.
(5) It reveals frauds committed by the staff handling cash and cheques and thus, helps the management to have effective control.

PART– II

9

Monitoring of Stock Statement

Commercial Banks finance mainly for working capital needs of their borrowers. This finance is meant to help the borrowers in building up a reasonable level of current assets and is secured by the underlying current assets, called primary security. Thus, a borrower is required to give details of assets build up at prescribed intervals to enable the bank to grant him authority to draw funds from the bank against the limit sanctioned to him. Assessment of the required level of finance is part of sanctioning process whereas ensuring an adequate level of assets to secure bank's finance is part of the process of follow up and supervision. An important tool for proper follow-up and supervision of advances is stock statement.

Stock-statement is the document which a borrower submits to his banker at prescribed periodicity, usually monthly, containing details of the current assets on the basis of which drawing power is given in the borrower's account to facilitate drawings from the account. Since it is current assets that are financed by working capital bankers and the current assets keep on changing in value, the stock statements are basically the statements of current assets, namely, stocks and debtors as on a particular date.

A borrower is required to maintain an adequate level of current assets at all times. However, it is not possible to verify it on a continuous basis. Therefore, submission of stock statement by borrower at prescribed intervals giving complete details of security forms part of expected financial discipline. If a borrower avoids or delays it, the banker should become circumspect. If the delay is repeated, the reasons should be thoroughly examined. Provisions are usually built into the terms and conditions of sanction of advantage to penalise delays in submission of stock statements by increasing the pricing of advance either directly by levying of mark up say 1 per cent, over the applicable interest rate or indirectly by affecting the credit risk rating of a borrower. Further, under the new Income Recognition and Asset Classification norms, an account is classified as a Non-Performing Asset if the last stock statement is more than 3 months old. It goes to suggest the importance of stock statements.

Calculation of Drawing Power

The drawing power is given only against saleable stocks and good debtors not older than a stated cover period, say 90 days. While calculating drawing power (DP), a certain percentage is deducted from stocks and debtors as margin which is supposed to be contributed by the borrower by way of net working capital and from other sources of finance like trade creditors. However, since outstandings against usance letters of credit are source of financing trade creditors by banks, these are deducted from the value of stocks. Similarly, bills discounted with banks are deducted from receivables if not excluded by the borrowers in their stock statements.

Usually, a margin of 25 per cent is prescribed for stocks and 40 per cent for receivables. However, sometimes, different margins may be fixed for different components of stocks by prescribing higher margin on semi-finished goods-may not be readily saleable at the stated cost.

The drawing power is calculated as under :

Value of stock	: S
Less Banker's acceptances (Outstanding usance letters of credit)	: BA
Less margin (Usually 25%)	: M_1=25% of (S–BA)
Advance value of stocks	: A_1=S–BA–M_1
Value of receivables	: R
Less bills discounted with banks	: BD
Less margin (usually 40%)	: M_2=40% of (R–BD)
Advance value of receivables	: A_2=R–BD–M_2
Total advance	
Value of security	: A=A_1+A_2
Limit sanctioned	: L
Drawing power	: Lower of A and L

Drawing power is value of security and the limit sanctioned whichever is lower.

Assuming that:-

(a) Value of stock Rs. 10,00,000

(b) Banker's acceptance Rs. 2,00,000

(c) Value of receivables Rs. 12,00,000

(d) Bills discounted with bank Rs. 2,00,000

Calculation of DP will be as under :-

S = Rs. 10,00,000

BA = Rs. 2,00,000

M_1 = Rs. 10,00,000–Rs. 2,00,000=Rs. 8,00,000
= 25% of Rs. 8,00,000 = Rs. 2,00,000

A_1 = Rs. 10,00,000–Rs. 2,00,000–Rs. 2,00,000
= Rs. 6,00,000

R = Rs. 12,00,000

BD = Rs. 2,00,000

M_2 = Rs. 12,00,000–Rs.2,00,000=Rs. 10,00,000
= 40% of Rs. 10,00,000= Rs. 4,00,000

A_2 = Rs. 12,00,000–Rs. 2,00,000–Rs. 4,00,000
= Rs. 6,00,000

$A = A_1 + A_2$

$= \text{Rs. } 6{,}00{,}000 + \text{Rs. } 6{,}00{,}000 – \text{Rs. } 12{,}00{,}000$

Drawing power is the lower of A and L. If limit sanctioned (L) is Rs. 10,00,000, DP will also be Rs. 10,00,000 only. If limit sanctioned (L) is Rs. 15,00,000 then DP will be Rs. 12,00,000 only.

The Issue of Trade Creditors

Two questions normally bother the minds of Credit Officers while calculating drawing power. Different banks approach the issues differently and the operating officials issue different instructions.

These are :

(i) Whether the trade creditor's should be deducted from chargeable asets while granting drawing power?

(ii) If yes, whether the creditors should be deducted before or after calculating the margin?

First issue is controversial and has not been settled conclusively. Some bankers deduct the trade creditors from chargeable assets on the plea that finance to that extent has been provided by the creditors and inclusion of such stocks for purpose of calculating drawing power would amount to double financing. However, the argument is relic of the era of credit rationing. Another argument is that since such stocks are unpaid for, banker's title to such goods may be doubtful. However, the Sale of Goods Act (Section 30 and 49) places clear title on banks in such stocks validly pledged/ hypothecated by the borrowers. Bank's title is doubtful only in case of goods in transit, which are either not included in stock statement or a suitable certificate declaring that the goods are not subject to any lien and the borrower possesses title to goods, is furnished by the borrower on the stock statement itself.

The moot point in the whole issue is that working capital bankers finance a borrower's Balance Sheet and not individual assets. It is a part of working capital gap that is sought to be finance by banks and a certain level of trade creditors is always factored into the calculations of this gap. Therefore, it is only when the actual level of trade creditors increases beyond the level envisaged at the time of assessment of limits that the trade creditors should be deducted, that too only the amount in excess of the projected level of trade creditors vis-a-vis the projected and actual level of sales turnover and trade creditors may be obtained from the borrower as on the date of stock statement.

Suppose,

Actual level of trade creditors = Ca

Ca = Rs. 10,00,000

Projected level of trade creditors = Cp

Cp = Rs. 8,00,000

Actual level of annualised sales = Sa

Sa = Rs. 6,00,000

Projected level of annual sales = Sp

Sp = Rs. 3,00,000

Then the amount of creditors (C) to be deducted from the advance value of security i.e. after calculating margins is given by,

C = Ca–Cp–Sa/Sp = Rs. 10,00,000–Rs. 8,00,000–Rs. 6,00,000 / Rs. 3,00,000

Hence C = 0

Thus, if the actual level of annualised sales is not much different from level projected for assessment of sanctioned limits and the actual creditors for exceed the projected level of creditors, then

C = Ca–Cp = Rs. 10,00,000–Rs. 8,00,000 = Rs. 2,00,000

If the excess creditors are not deducted above, the borrower may be tempted to divert excess funds available.

But the down side of this is that if the level of creditors falls below the projected level, then more finance will be needed. More bank finance can not be immediately available because of formalities of sanction of enhanced limits and legal documentation. Therefore, the borrower is expected to realistically project the availability of trade credit.

It may be noted that if the Net Working Capital (NWC), i.e., the excess of current assets over currect liabilities or funds brought from long term sources to finance currect assets, matches or exceeds the margin requirement, then deducting trade creditors would not result into shortage of working capital with the borrower. However, this was supposed to be the case when the concept of Maximum Permissible Bank Finance (MPBF) and Current Ratio (CR) of 1.33 were in operation under the Tandon/Chore Committee norms. With the demise of MPBF and adoption of flexible approach in acceptable Current Ratio, the issue of trade creditors has gained importance. Under the New Flexible Approach, the required margin may be provided partly by NWC and partly by Trade Creditors where Current Ratio of less than 1.33 is accepted and a margin of 25 per cent is stipulated (assuming the margin to be uniform for stocks and debtors).

So long as the sum of NWC and trade creditors equals the margin requirement, the borrower would be able to avail full sanctioned limit. But, if the sum of NWC and trade creditors falls short of margin requirement, the account would show irregularity (i.e. overdrawing). If, on the other hand, the sum of NWC and trade creditors exceeds the margin requirement, then the borrower would need less funds than the sanctioned limit but it would be free to utilise the full limit. In this situation, either the limit would remain under-utilised or some of the trade creditors would be paid-off or funds would be diverted into other uses leading to reduction in NWC and CR. In fact, diversion of funds and reduction in NWC is possible in all the above situations. Many a time it may happen that the NWC has been severely eroded or has even become negative and the entire margin comes from trade creditors. In this case, the CR will be close to or less than one. This is extremely risky and, therefore, it must be ensured that the borrower maintains an acceptable level of NWC and CR. To pressurise a borrower to bring the actual level of NWC to the acceptable level, the drawing power may be calculated by deducting excess creditors before calculating margins. Given an acceptable level of NWC and Current Ratio, the trade creditors should not be deducted from chargeable current assets for the purpose of granting drawing power in the account. However, banker's acceptances and Usance Letter of Credit outstanding, against which goods have been received and included in the stock statement, must be deducted since these are separately financed by the lending banks.

Verification of Stock Statement

The drawing power in an account may be given on the basis of the stock statement submitted by the borrower unless there are reasons to believe that the stock statement does not contain correct information. Thereafter, it may be verified as early as possible. In the case of small borrowers, stock statements can be easily verified thoroughly. But in the case of large borrowers, a thorough scrutiny is impossible keeping in view the time required for such an effort. For example, a borrower may be having manufacturing facilities at three different locations and may be keeping stocks at fifty different sales depots in different parts of the country. Obviously, if the level of operation of a borrower is very large and the stocks are stored at different locations, the same may be verified at irregular intervals keeping in mind the relative proportion of such stocks in the total value of stocks. While on physical verification, it should be verified whether the actual position of stocks matches the position given in the stock statement. It is normally recommended that the items mentioned in the stock statement may be verified by

ABC analysis or on a random sample basis. Some invoices may be checked for price verification and account statements of some major customers may be taken to verify whether the debtors are correctly stated and whether these lie within the prescribed cover period.

A Tool for Financial Follow-up

Next logical question is what other things to look for in a stock statement and how to scrutinise it ? Before answering this question, however, one needs to know what purposes the stock statement may serve. Undoubtedly, the prime purpose of stock statement is to calculate the level upto which the borrower may draw from the sanctioned limits. However, it also serves as a potent tool for proper follow-up and supervision of advances. Bank's follow-up and super-vision of advances involves physical inspection as well as financial follow-up. Stock Statement is one document which may be used for both the purposes. Towards physical inspection, it is the basis for verification of actual levels of individual items of current assets. Towards financial follow-up, it can be used to look specifically for the following aspects:

1. Whether bank's finance has been put to proper end use by building up sufficient level of current assets to support the actual outstandings in the account. It will also ensure that bank's advance is fully secured.

2. Whether the level of current assets maintained by the borrower is sufficient to achieve the projected level of turnover. A business is run on a particular operation cycle which cannot be constrained by lack of proper levels of stocks and debtors.

3. Whether there are non-moving/old/obsolete/returned/rejected stocks and old debtors which might have turned unrecoverable. The borrowers have a tendency of financing such items from bank's funds.

4. Whether the operating cycle is functioning as envisaged and there are no glitches in the production or trading process. It may happen that some items of current assets are more and others are less than the levels required for smooth functioning of operations.

5. Whether the borrower is reporting correct level of stocks, debtors and creditors. In an anxiety to avail of more finance from banks, some borrowers may be tempted to include those items in Stock Statement which were agreed to be excluded or certain items may be just inflated.

6. Whether the borrower is inflating sales by booking false sales. To artificially show achievement of envisaged sales target, some borrowers may resort to booking purchase and sale of same item with some other firm in need of similar types of transactions.

Precautions while Scrutinising Stock Statements

A borrower may not be reporting correct figures in the stock statement to hide diversion of funds. The diversion of funds may be hidden by overstating stocks and debtors or by understating creditors. Diverted funds may also be shown as advance payments for material and included in stock statement to avail of enhanced drawing power in the account.

Following are some of the major areas for verification to ensure that borrowers do not indulge in irregular practices:

1. Stock should be valued as per the method adopted for the purpose of previous annual financial statement or at lower of the market price, actual cost and invoice value less rebate/discount. However, the value shown in the Stock Statement may be higher than this price to avail of higher finance or hide the irregularity in the account.

2. Stock Statement may include non moving/non saleable/old/obsolete/returned/rejected stocks.

3. Including bad debts and those beyond the accepted cover period in trade debtors. Care should be taken that debtors do not include other than trade debtors.

4. Showing stocks in transit when there are none. Otherwise also, the goods in transit have to be very carefully viewed as regards their value and an appropriate declaration by the borrower regarding valid title to such goods. An exercise in comparison of such goods with previous stock statements would be fruitful.

5. Showing diverted funds as advance payment for material . Such amounts may be substantial and outstanding for a long time. In one case, a large borrower was found to be actually showing a large amount as advance payment to different suppliers to hide diversion of funds.

6. Showing more than normal inventory as Work in Process (WIP). Since most of the borrowers do not maintain verifiable record and valuation systems for WIP, actual verification becomes difficult. To take advantage of this problem, borrowes may show such stocks at inflated levels.

7. Some borrowers may be found showing comparatively larger inventory at Stock Statement dates and maintaining lower levels on other days.

But why would a borrower need to do all this ? Obviously, if the business is run as envisaged, there should not be any reason to camouflage the stock statements and avail higher finance from banks. The fact is that some borrowers still do it. The major motive comes from the temptation to divert bank's short term funds into those medium and long term uses for which term lenders may not extend term finance, for example, intercorporate investments. Also, the business may be incurring losses eating into its NWC in the absence of infusion of long term funds. To hide depletion in NWC, the current assets may be shown at inflated value. Other motives could be financing debtors beyond the cover period, bad debts, useless inventory, etc., before any unrecoverable item is charged to Profit and Loss Account to avoid affecting the profitability of business in its annual financial statements. The least common but not uncommon reason could be outright withdrawal of funds from the business without the knowledge of the financing bank.

Finally, the basic idea while scrutinising and verifying a Stock Statement should be to ensure that the borrower is neither under-financed nor over-financed, since both the situations would be harmful for the borrower and the bank. Therefore, there is no need to be either too overcautious or too lax in one's approach. The approach should always be realistic and reasonable keeping in mind the fact that running businesses are dynamic entities facing quite uncertain situations.

10

The Concept of Capital Adequacy Ratio for PSBs

Capital is a common parlance means shareholder's money. However, in the context of banking and minimum capital requirement, it has a broader perspective Tier I capital accounting for shareholders money and Tier II consisting of additional resources both external and internal available to the bank. The bank has to hold at least half of its measured capital in Tier I form. Adequacy is related to the risks a banking company undertakes in its asset creation-be it credit risk, operational risk, market risk etc. Capital is necessary for banks as a caution against losses and it provided an incentive for owners of business to manage it in a prudent manner bank capital plays a critical role in the safety and soundness of individual banks and the banking system.

Capital Adequacy Ratio is defined as a ratio of capital to risk weighted assets. It is important to note that the capital requirement applies to assets and the reserve requirement applies to liabilities. The reserve requirements impose a lower limit on the amount of reserves a bank must own relative to demand deposits of its customers. Capital requirement limits the total amount of credit a bank may issue. Low (credit) risk assets like cash have a zero per cent risk, weighted capital requirement and claims on commercial companies have a 100 per cent risk weight.

The first Capital Adequacy requirement for banks in India was in 1961 when RBI instructed banks to maintain a 6 per cent capital to its total deposits.

The period of four years 1992 to 1996 and thereafter has seen a dramatic improvement in Capital Adequacy Ratios (CAR) in Indian banking sector.

For the public sector banks this has been possible mainly due to Government capital infusion, which has accounted for nearly 75 per cent of total capital accretion, the balance being made up by revaluation of assets, profits of World Bank loan and public issue. As on 31/03/96,19 out of 27 public sector banks had reached the 8 per cent CAR, of the remaining 8, two showed negative CAR around an average of 6 per cent.

The constraints faced by the public sector banks in reaching the 8 per cent CAR have been mainly -

- The new income recognition and asset classification norms.
- The rising quantum in providing depreciation on Govt. Securities held for SLR purpose.
- The tax rules, which don't permit deduction of provisions on non-performing assets for calculating income tax.
- The social orientation, which affected the profit earning capacity of most of public sector banks.
- Local governmental pressures on directed lending, continuance of unviable branches.
- The impressive branch expansion from 8262 in 1969 to over 60000 in 2004 having resulted in heavier overheads. This burden has presented banks from building up a healthy reserves portfolio.
- The awareness of the concept of capital adequacy and its future implications on the bank being confined to the department concerned.

Capital Adequacy is a dynamic concept closely related to performance of a bank, and it is parameter for evaluation under CAMEL. In future, banks cannot afford to have a haphazard growth in assets and consequently liabilities as their Capital Adequacy would come under pressure. Though RBI has not spelt out the repercussions of not reaching the adequacy requirements, those may in general affects the operational functions adversely, which ultimately would affect the bottom line.

The Narsimham committee II has recommended that CAR for all banks in India should be 9 per cent by the year 2005 and 10 per cent thereafter which will require additional capital by almost all public sector commercial banks.

$$\text{Capital Adequacy} = \frac{\text{Total Capital}}{\text{Credit Risk + Market Risk + Operational Risk}}$$

This is presently 8 per cent as prescribed by Basel (The minimum prescribed rate by RBI is 9 per cent)

Example: Suppose, Total capital = Rs. 500, Market risk = Rs. 10, Operational risk = Rs. 20.

Denominator of CAR = 500 + {(10 + 20) × 12.5} = Rs. 875

However, banks will have to provide capital resources for operational risk by keeping aside a substantial portion of gross income (8 per cent of 15 per cent of gross income).

The capital requirement will also be 8 per cent as against existing level maintained by most of banks, which is above 10 per cent of the risk weighted assets.

11

Assessment of Working Capital Need for SSI Unit

Working capital for any manufacturing unit means the total amount of circulating funds required for the continuous operation of the unit on an ongoing basis. For an uninterrupted functioning of a unit at a given capacity it requires a specific level of current assets, namely raw materials, stock-in-progress or stock-in-process, finished goods, receivables apart from reasonable cash in hand etc. these forms the operating cycle of the unit.

The working capital operating cycle of a manufacturing unit can be represented by the following diagram:

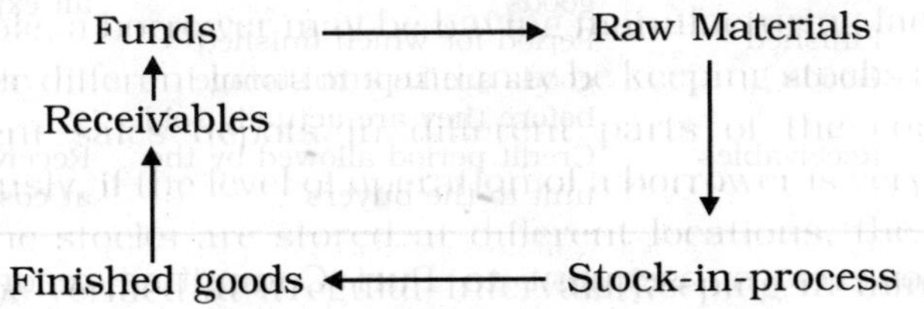

This means that there are four distinct stages of working capital cycles which are as under:

(1) Funds (whether own or borrowings) are utilised for purchase of raw materials.

(2) Raw materials are converted into finished goods.

(3) Finished goods are stored in the godown before they are sold.

(4) Finished goods are sold on credit and converted into accounts receivables or sundry debtors which, when realised are converted into funds and the process recycles itself.

Thus, in order to find out the total working capital requirement of a SSI Unit, the needs at each of the four stages mentioned above are calculated and the sum total thereof is its total working capital requirement.

However, in order to arrive at each of four stages the banker is to assess two parameters with reference to each stage:

(1) Time factor

(2) Value

These parameters of various stages can be enumerated as under:

Stage	*Item*	*Time*	*Value*
I	Raw material	Consumption storage period of raw material	Value of raw materials for the period
II	Stock-in-process	Time taken to convert the raw materials into finished goods	Raw material consumed + all expenses
III	Finished Goods	Period for which finished goods are kept in storage before they are actually sold	do
IV	Receivables	Credit period allowed by the unit to the buyers	Receivables at cost

However, subsequent to Puri Committee recommendations, the procedure of assessment of working capital of an SSI unit has been rationalised.

(A) Assessment of Working Capital upto Rs. 25,000

Working capital required for such units can be computed by the single formula as under -

Working Capital = B × D / 30

Where B = Total expenditure during the month

D = Total number of days in the working capital cycle.

Notes:

(a) The total expenditure during the month comprises of the followings:

- Raw materials/stores/spares
- Wages and salaries
- Drawings for sustenance of proprietor/partners
- Other expenses like rent, depreciation etc.

(b) Total number of days will comprise of the sum total of number of days at each of the four stages of the working capital cycle as discussed earlier.

(c) Since no margin is to be obtained for credit facilities up to and inclusive of Rs. 25,000 under all SSI schemes, the total amount calculated above can be released to the borrower subject to, however, creating charge on the assets created out of the loan amount.

Assuming that—

Stage	*Item*	*Time*	*Value (Rs.)*
I	Raw material	2 days	1,00,000
II	Stock-in-process	7 days	1,00,000 + 20,000 = 1,20,000
III	Finished goods	10 days	- Do -
IV	Receivables	8 days	- Do -
	Total	27 days	

Working capital required will be = 1,20,000 × 27 / 30
= Rs. 1,08,000

(B) Assessment of Working Capital ranging between Rs. 25,000 and Rs. 2,00,000

In such accounts the total working capital requirement is calculated by adding the values at column 4. Now

Permissible Bank Finance (PBF) can easily be assessed as under-

Item (1)	*Working Capital (2)*	*Margin (%) (3)*	*Value (4)*	*PBF (2–4)*
Raw materials				
Stock-in-process				
Finished goods				
Receivables				
Expenses				
Total				
Less liquid surplus available in a/c as on......				
Less credit on purchases				
Limits recom-mended or MPBF				

Notes:

(a) Though assessment of working capital should be need-based as calculated above, release of the same will be security oriented, i.e. allowing withdrawals as for available D.P. based on stock statements to be submitted by the borrower.

(b) Liquid surplus as per Balance Sheet will be difference between the current assets and current liabilities. However, deficit, if any (i.e. if current liabilities are more than current assets), should be added to the total working capital requirement.

12

Management of Working Capital

Working Capital may be regarded as the life blood of the business. Its effective provision can do much to ensure the success of a business. Efficiency in the management of working capital has always been appreciated by the well-run enterprises from the point of view of both profitability and viability. If the working capital is not managed efficiently, the flow of funds (money) get choked, raw materials supplies interrupted, wage payment delayed, clamour for clearance of other outstanding expenses gather momentum; all of them leading to a virtual stoppage of operations. Hence, the management of working capital is one of the important aspect of overall financial management. It is necessary for enterprises to maintain satisfactory level of working capital. The management of working capital basically involves three processes: anticipated needed funds, acquiring funds and monitoring and balancing constituent elements of working capital.

Every business need funds for two purposes. Long-term funds are required to create production facilities through purchase of fixed assets, such as plant and machinery, land, building etc. Investments in these assets represent that part of firm's capital which is blocked on a permanent or fixed basis and is called fixed assets. Funds are also needed for short-term purposes for the purchase of raw materials, payment of wages and other day-to-day expenses etc. These funds are known as working capital. This working capital is also known as a revolving or circulatory capital or short-term capital.

The Financial Manager is always interested in obtaining working capital at the right time, at a reasonable cost and at the best favourable terms. Commercial banks are the principal source of working capital. They provide working capital in the form of overdrafts, cash-credit, short-term loans, bills financing, bank guarantee etc. The banks provide working capital at the manufacturing level (pre-sale stage for acquisition/holding required level of inventory). The inventory finance remained secured with current assets primarily and repaid out of sales process of goods manufactured. Inventory finance is generally extended by way of cash credit either against hypothecation or pledge or both. The Reserve Bank of India has withdrawn its entire prescription relating to the Maximum Permissible Bank Finance (MPBF) system of assessment of working capital requirements of any firm pursuing the policy of deregulation of the banking sector. Except in a few cases, the banks are free to evolve their own policy in the matter of working capital assessments of their borrowers and have such policies approved by their Board of Directors.

Concept of Working Capital

There are two concepts of working capital - Gross working capital and Net working capital. The gross working capital, generally, refers as investments in current assets such as marketable securities, inventories and bills receivables etc. Current assets are those assets which are normally converted into cash within a year. The term "net working capital" refers the difference between the current assets and current liabilities. Current liabilities are those claims of the outsiders which are expected to mature for payment within one year and include creditors, bills payable, bank overdraft and expenses outstanding. This net working capital may be positive or negative. When current assests are more than current liabilities the net working capital becomes positive and whereas the current liabilities exceed current assets, the net working capital becomes negative.

Dangers of Inadequate Working Capital

When the working capital is inadequate, a firm may face the following problems:

1. It may not be able to take advantage of cash discounts.
2. It cannot buy its raw materials requirements in bulk and unable to utilise the optimum benefit of production facilities.
3. It may not be able to take advantage of profitable business opportunities.
4. Its low liquidity may lead to low profitability. In the same way, low profitability result in low liquidity.
5. Short term liabilities cannot be paid because of inadequate working capital. This may lead to borrow funds at an exorbitant rate of interest.
6. Credit-worthiness of the firm may be damaged because of lack of liquidity resulting in losing the credit-worthiness of the firm.
7. Low liquidity may lead to winding up of the firm due to inability to meet out its debt-obligations.
8. Fixed Assets cannot efficiently and effectively be utilised on account of lack of sufficient working capital.

Dangers of Excessive Working Capital

Excessive working capital raises the following problems:

1. A firm may be tempted to over trade and lose heavily.
2. The situation may lead to unnecessary purchases and accumulation of inventories. This may cause chances of theft, waste and losses etc.

3. There may arise an imbalance between liquidity and profitability.
4. Excessive working capital means that the funds are idle. When funds are idle, no profit is earned. When it is so, the rate of return on its investment goes down.
5. The situation may lead to greater production which may lead to over supply and crash of the prices.
6. Excessive working capital may lead to carelessness of cost of production.

Factors Determining Working Capital

It is necessary for any organisation to run successfully its affairs has to provide for adequate working capital. Managing working capital requires more attention than managing plant and equipment expenditure. Mismanagement of working capital can be costly. Too large an investment in working capital means tying up capital that can be used productively elsewhere. On the other hand, too little investment in inventory and working capital may also be expensive due to loss of sales. The exact forecast of the working capital is important and is dependant on the following factors:

1. Production policies. The production policies pursued by the management have a significant effect on the requirements of working capital of any business. The production schedule has a great influence on the level of inventories, payment of wages to labourers and the overheads. In case of labour intensive industries the working capital requirements are more than the automatic plants. Sometimes changes in technology may lead to improvement in processing of raw-materials, savings in wastages, greater productivity and more speedy production. All these improvements may reduce investment in inventory and wages.

2. Nature of business. Working capital also depends upon the nature of the business. The industries where most of the transactions are on cash basis need very little working capital. On the other hand, ordinary manufacturing and trading concerns require larger working capital since they have to invest substantially in inventories, wages and debtors.

3. Length in the period of process. Larger the period of process of the raw materials, the higher will be the requirement of the working capital and vice-versa. That is why high capital intensive and longer manufacturing period oriented industries need large amount of working capital in comparison to small trading concerns where the process period is nil or short. An utmost care should be taken to shorten the period of processing in order to minimise the working capital requirement.

4. Credit policies. A firm, which allows credit to its customers, need more working capital as compared to a firm which has strict credit terms. It is observed that the firm who used to allow credit to its customers liberally, clocks more sales than the other who has strict credit terms but in the former case a substantial amount of working capital will be tied up in its sundry debtors or bills receivables. The working capital requirement can also be affected by credit facilities enjoyed by its suppliers. Those firms which enjoyed liberal credit facilities need less working capital than the others.

5. Working capital rotations. Working capital has a rotational cycle, i.e., cash, raw material, processing, finished goods, debtors and cash. Those firms with a shorter period of rotational cycle need lower working capital and vice-versa.

6. Seasonal fluctuations. Some industries have seasonal manufacturing and selling process. For example, sugar and woollen textile industries. These industries need working capital substantially in the season when they manufacture and have a larger cash flow during the selling season. A sugar unit produces all the sugar between

December to April every year and requires higher working capital during this period as compared to any other period. Cyclical changes in the economy also influence quantum of working capital. In period of boom, i.e., when the business is prosperous, there is need of large working capital due to increase in sales, rise in output prices and future prospectus. In a recession though the working capital funds are required but to be locked into unsold inventories and debtors.

7. Fluctuations of supply. Some industries and trading concerns have to maintain larger inventories due to their irregular sales and intermitted supply. This is particularly true in the case of firms requiring special kind of raw-materials availing only from one or two sources. In such cases large amount of raw materials has to the kept in store to avoid any possibility of the production process coming to dead halt. As such working capital requirements of such firms may be large.

Tools Determining Working Capital

The most ticklish problem that an enterprise or banker is faced is the determination of the amount of working capital required at a particular level of business operation. The working capital can be forecast after taking into account the following tools:

1. Fund Flow Statement of the firm.
2. Cash flow statement of the firm.
3. Financial statement of the firm.
4. Ratio analysis.

1. Fund Flow Statement: This statement measures the inflows and outflows of net working capital that result from any type of business activity. According to the Inter-national Accounting Standard No. 7 “Funds” generally refers to cash and cash equivalents or to working capital. The fund flow statement is widely used by the bankers and financial managers in performance of their jobs. It has become a useful tool in their analytical kit. This is because the financial statements - Balance Sheet and Profit and Loss Account statement have a limited role to perform due to their static nature. Balance Sheet is a statement of assets and liabilities as on a particular date. It does not focus those major financial transactions, which have been behind the Balance Sheet changes. One has to draw inferences from the Balance Sheet about other major financial transaction only after comparing the Balance Sheet of two periods. By comparing the two Balance Sheets and Profit and Loss Accounts, the financial analyst may draw, an inference regarding the sources and application of the funds.

The fund flow statement has wide uses in inferring the financial position of the firm and future working capital of the firm. It helps us to know why the liquid position of the business is becoming more and more unbalanced in spite of business being profitable and why the business could have good liquid position in spite of business making losses. Hence, it can infer the sources and use the funds in a better way. The projection of the fund flow statement will help the banker or the analyst in finding out how the management is going to allocate the recourses for meeting the productive requirement of the business. The entrepreneur may use the scarce resources to the best use of the enterprises and may fulfill the business commitment in time.

2. Cash flow statement: This statement measures inflows and outflows of cash on account of any type of business activity depicting change in cash position from one period to another. It helps management in making plans for the immediate future. A proper projection of the cash flow statement will enable management to meet out his commitment in time and to use the surplus cash for productive purpose. Cash flow projections are prepared taking into account the sources and applications of the cash for two different periods usually for one year. The difference between fund flow statement and the cash flow statement is that the fund flow statement is concerned with changes in working capital between the two Balance Sheets whereas the cash flow statement is concerned with the changes in cash balances which is only the one constituent of the working capital. Cash flow statement is a tool of financial analysis of working capital in a short period. It is useful for short - term planning. The shorter the period coverd by the analysts, the greater is the importance of cash flow analysis. However, cash flow statement may not represent the real liquid position of the business and the inferences may be obtained by analyzing fund flow and income statement alongwith cash flow statement. In fact, cash flow discloses the volume as well as the speed at which the cash flows in different segments of the business. Indian banks are assessing the working capital of sugar, tea, construction and software and information technology industry by adopting cash budget/ cash flow approach. Assessment of working capital based on cash flow is best suited for considering sanction of adhoc facilities or seasonal business.

3. Financial Statements: The financial statements generally refers to two basic statements, i.e., Profit and Loss Account or Income Statement and Balance Sheet. Profit and Loss Account shows what has happened to the business due to operations between two Balance Sheet dates. The earning capacity and potential of the firm are reflected by the Profit and Loss Account. It presents the summary of revenue, expenses and net income/loss of a firm for a period. The entrepreneur always keeps an eye on the returns from investment and the Profit/Loss is of utmost importance for him to know whether the business is conducted on sound terms or not.

As such a Balance Sheet reflects the financial position of a firm on a particular date. It is a pictorial presentation of financial health of the business, i.e., resources and liabilities on a particular date. The important distinction between an Income Statement and Balance Sheet is that the Income

Statement is for a period whereas balance sheet is on a particular date. Both the above financial statements are important for decision making for entrepreneur and banker. Financial statements are analysed and interpreted by different persons in different ways to assess the earning capacity, progress, debt-repaying capacity. Efficiency of operation and future, plans/progress of the firm.

4. Ratio analysis: Balance Sheet and Income Statements are static and need to be arranged and interpreted for assessment of strength and weaknesses of the firm. Ratio analysis is an important and age-old technique of financial analysis of Balance Sheet and Income Statements. It is useful to number of parties, i.e., entrepreneurs, creditors, bankers, shareholders and executives of the firm. The most important ratios for assessing and financing the working capital are liquidity and solvency ratio which includes:

(a) Current ratio
(b) Liquid ratio
(c) Absolute liquid ratio
(d) Proprietorship ratio
(e) Capital gearing ratio
(f) Stock turnover ratio
(g) Net working capital ratio.

Ratio analysis simplifies the comprehension of financial statement and helps in planning and forecasting the working capital. It also provides clues on trend and future problems.

The RBI has announced that Maximum Permissible Bank Finance (MPBF) concept is not mandatory with effect from April 1997 and has put the Bankers to follow their own assessment for effective working capital of a firm. Banker as well as borrower has to work with mutual trust in arriving at the correct level of working capital by using the tools and the factors determining the working capital because excessive and inadequate working capital may hamper the business and the productivity of the firm.

13

Bank Credit and Limitation Period for Filing Suits in Courts of Law

Banks are required to finance various sectors e.g., agriculture, industry, SSI and other non-priority sector advances. They are also required to finance under various Government sponsored schemes such as PMRY, SEPUP, SUME, POP and IRDP etc. Apart from it bank also finance for consumer loans, vehicle loans, housing loans, education loans etc., to public and its staff. Banks are required to fulfill the target of finance according to the directions of Reserve Bank of India and the Central Government based on national economic policy.

While ascertaining a credit proposal a banker, apart from examining the viability, has to ensure the enforceability of the securities, all the terms and conditions are reduced in writing as it identifies the borrower, properties, nature of facilities, charge, terms and conditions and limitation period. If the borrower commits a default in repayment or any other terms and conditions the bank has a right to proceed legally by filing suit in the courts of law. The right of filing suit in courts of law is derived from the documents.

It would be seen that the plaintiff can not wait for unlimited time and is allowed to file suit as and when he desires. The defendant cannot be put to peril any time, the plaintiff desires. If this is allowed there shall be complete mess of the legal jurisprudence. Moreover, it is the intention of the legislative that law helps the diligent and not the indolent.

Indian Limitation Act has prescribed certain period within which a suit can be filed in the courts of law as per Section 3 of the Limitation Act any suit if filed after expiry of limitation period shall be dismissed.

Limitation Period at a glance:-

	Type of Documents	*Period of Limitation*
1.	D.P. note	3 years from the date of execution
2.	Bill of exchange or D.P. note	3 years from the date when it falls due
3.	Bill of exchange payable at sight or after sight	3 years from the date when default is made
4.	Temporary overdraft	3 years from the date of debit in the account
5.	Promissory note of articles of agreement payable by instalments, which provides that, if default is made in payment of any or more instalments, the whole shall become due.	3 years from the date when default is made
6.	Letter of guarantee	3 years from the date of demand on the guarantor
7.	Pledge/hypothecation agreements	3 years from the date of execution
8.	Mortgages	
	(a) Money payable on demand	12 years from the date of mortgage
	(b) If amount payable by instalment	12 years from the date when default is made
	(c) Personal liability on a mortagage	3 years from the date of execution of mortgage deed

It may be noted that in computing the period of limitation, the day from which such period shall be reckoned, shall be excluded.

Guarantors and the Law of Limitation

The law of limitation in respect of guarantors is highly complicated and not free from controversies because the law of limitation does not expressly provide any period or limitation for a suit against the guarantors. There are number of different and contradictory judgements of different courts.

As per section 128, Indian Contract Act, the liability of the surety and Guarantor is co-extensive with that the principal debtor unless it is otherwise provided by the contract. Thus, generally the guarantee provides that the payment by the guarantor is to be made on demand by the creditor. So, the guarantor should be called upon to pay the amount stating that the borrower has failed to repay the loan. It is worth noting that the limitation period starts against the guarantor only from the date of demand from him. It may be noted that the limitation period against the guarantor is three years from the date when the cause of action accrues against him i.e.; from the date of demand or death, insolvency or the revocation of guarantee by the guarantor.

The general proposition of law is that when a borrower executes documents afresh or acknowledges the debt before the expiry of limitation period, the limitation not only extends against the borrower but against the guarantor also. Supreme Court in the case of Margaret Lalita Sanyal *Vs.* Indo Commercial Bank Ltd. A/R 1976 SC 102, observed that as the guarantee is continuing guarantee and the undertaking by the defendant is to pay any amount that may be due by the company at the root of general balance of its account or any other account. Whatsoever if the account is alive account and there is no refusal on the part of the guarantor to carry out the obligation, we do not see how the period of limitation could be said to have commenced running. Limitation would run only from the date of breach under Article 115 of the schedule of the Limitation Act 1908.

In the case of Bombay Dyeing and Mfg. Co. Ltd *Vs.* State Bank of Bombay 1958 SCR 1122 it was held by the Supreme Court that ever though the suit against the debtor is barred by limitation, the creditor is entitled to recover the debt from surety.

In the case of Union Bank of India *Vs.* T.J. Steliers and others (1989) 66 Company cases Kerala 96, it was held that in case of continuing guarantee so long as the guarantee has not been withdrawn or so long as the guarantors have not refused to perform their obligation under the agreement of guarantee and a suit has not been filed within the prescribed period of limitation the guarantors are liable under the agreement for the amounts found due to the creditor from the principal debtor.

Provision Relating to Extension of Limitation Period

Although the law of limitation is specific and well prescribed yet this is most complicated issue so far as filing of suits by the bank is concerned. Normally the documents should be renewed invariably before the expiry of the original documents but it has been seen that generally the branches ignore this aspect and are at their wits end when the account goes bad and bank has to file suit, they get confused and many a times discrepancies crept in the suit/ plaint which are likely to damage the interests of the bank. So it is in the interest of the banks that they should maintain a register in which date of expiry of documents in each loan account may be mentioned. This will provide the limitation period at a glance, which will facilitate the bank branch to get the documents renewed in time.

Though it is desirable that the documents should get renewed within the period of limitation the fact remains that the bank branches seldom care to get the documents renewed within time. Available information has revealed that in 87.4% cases the bank branches did not renew the documents in time, yet the bank gets the grace period for filing suit by virtue of Sections 18 and 19 of the Limitation Act.

Sections 18 and 19 of the Indian Limitation Act deals with the effect of acknowledgement in writing and the effect of repayment on account of debt or of interest on legacy. Where before the expiry of the existing limitation period an acknowledgement of liability is made in writing or account is stated and signed by the person who is liable or his duly authorised agent on his behalf, a fresh period of limitation shall be computed from the time when the acknowledgement stated was so signed.

It would be seen that the limitation is extended under the following circumstances:

- **Renewal of Documents**

The best way to get the limitation period is that the documents should be got renewed before the expiry of limitation period. When documents are renewed before the expiry of limitation fresh period of limitation starts from the date of execution of documents. This is the most authentic and desirable method to get the limitation period extended.

- **Balance Confirmation Letters**

The most popular and prominent method of extension of limitation period is by way of getting the balance confirmation letters. It has been provided in the Limitation Act that where before the expiry of prescribed period the party signs the balance confirmation; the period gets extended from the date of execution of such balance confirmation. Such acknowledgement must be in writing and signed by the person against whom the right of property is claimed. In the case of Bank of India *Vs.* Jems Fernandez A/R 1988 Kerala 89, it was held that there is nothing in Section 18 to indicate the legislative intent that the acknowledgement must be written in the hand of maker, ever if not written in his own hand writing is a valid acknowledgement capable of extending the period of limitation. In the Union Bank of India *Vs.* S.B. Mehta 11(1998) B C 23 Gujrat High Court, in this case the borrower obtained loan from the bank. The Guarantor alleged that even if this may be legal with respect to the borrower, the period of limitation is not extended against him. The court held that the period of limitation would be the same in respect of Principal and the Guarantor.

- **Cash Payment in the Account**

Where payment on account of debt is made before expiry of existing limitation period by a person liable to pay or his authorised agent under his signatures, a fresh period of limitation shall be computed from the date when the payment is made. Any payment in the account under the signature of the person authorised for operation in the account amounts to acknowledgement of liability. Such payment should be made by debtor himself and not by a third party unless expressly authorised by the debtor. So the payment by the debtor or his authorised agent provides a valid method to get the extended limitation period.

- **Acknowledgement in Balance Sheet**

Acknowledgement of debt by debtor in their balance sheets is a valid acknowledgement and extends the period of limitation from the date of Balance sheet.

- **Revival of Documents**

When a debt has become time barred, obtaining a fresh D.P. note can revive such a debt. This is based on the principle contained in Section 23(3) of the Indian Contract Act in past consideration. Thus, if a letter of linkage along-with a fresh D.P. note or set of documents is obtained from the debtor, it will give a fresh right to the creditor against the debtor.

14

Filing of Suits - Limitation

Banks are required to finance various sectors e.g. agriculture, SSI, non-priority, industry etc. Banks are required to fulfill, the target of finance according to directions of Reserve Bank of India and the Government. They are also required to finance under various government-sponsored schemes such as PMRY, SEPUP, SUME, and IRDP etc.

Banks grant loans to these sectors with the hope that it will be repaid as per schedule and terms of the loan agreement. But defaults do take place more often in these loans since generally the borrowers are not required to furnish any guarantee and security under these government sponsored schemes with a view to uplift the down-trodden and the needy, the government also provides subsidy under these schemes, sometimes, the borrowers take undue advantage of these privileges and become willful defaulters. The loan waiver schemes of the Central and State Governments also proved as a fuel to the fire in increasing number of willful defaulters.

Every suit and application shall be filed, preferred and made within the period of limitation as prescribed under the Limitation Act 1983. Care and caution must be exercised to ensure that the recovery of debts due to the bank and the enforceability of related securities do not get time barred. Else, the bank will be left without any remedy.

When file of suits or recovery proceedings is necessitated proposals should be moved well in advance by the Branch Manager to get sanction from the appropriate Higher Authority. As soon as the sanction is received, further action must be taken without any loss of time to ensure the filing of suit/ proceedings in time. Suits/ proceedings should be properly pursued and followed by delinquently in Bank's interest.

In case of the defendents or respondents dies during the pendency of the case in court, his legal representatives have to be brought on record; otherwise the case shall abate.

Central Principles/ Provisions that Decide Limitation

It is necessary to keep in mind for bankers the following points while determining limitation.

- There is a period of limitation 3 years in general and 12 years for mortgaged properties/ suits.
- There is a date from which limitation starts running. In case of demand pronote (Demand Loan), it is from the date of pronote. In case of cash-credit/ overdraft agreement it is from the date of documents/ agreements. In general, this date is the date on which the amount falls due and payable.
- In case of loans where repayment has been agreed to on instalment basis (Term Loans) the period of limitation will start from the date of respective defaults in terms of stipulations made in this behalf in the relative documents.
- A duly stamped acknowledgement of borrower will give a fresh start of limitation provided it is acknowledged before expiry of limitation.
- Similarly a part-payment of debt will give a fresh start of limitation provided it is paid before expiry of limitation and under the signature(s) of borrower(s) himself/ herself.

If the debt gets time-barred, the proper course would be to take an agreement/ promise to pay the said debts known as Letter of Revival.

The Balance and Security Confirmation Letter (BC) is acknowledgement of debt should be taken from the borrowers) and/ or guarantor(s) as the case may be, at the close of each half year or at such regular intervals as may be prescribed by the Bank. In case of protested advances separate form of B/C is in use.

Procedure for Obtaining B/C Letter

The Balance and Security Confirmation Letter obtained periodically from the borrowers as well as from the guarantors should be recorded in Balance Confirmation Documents Register. The signature of the borrower should be verified by an authorised official and rubber stamp affixed on the letter "Signature verified".

The date and place of execution of Balance and Security Confirmation Letters should be filled in by the borrowers themselves and not by any member of staff.

B/C Letters in Partnership Accounts

In case of partnership firm, B/C letters may be obtained from any partner unless there is anything to the contrary to the same in the partnership deed or the relative account opening form. In case the firm stands dissolved, it is preferable to obtain signature of all partners on the B/C letter till the account is adjusted in full.

B/C Letters in Guaranteed Accounts

At present in PNB guarantee is taken on PNB 58 (old 295) or PNB 785, para 9 of PNB 58 has a clause enabling the borrowers to confirm balance on behalf of guarantors. It is advisable to take B/C letters from guarantor also as a matter of abundant caution especially in case of higher limits.

These have been variance of opinion in different judgments of various courts regarding the validity of obtaining B/C letters from borrower only. As such it is preferable to obtain B/C letters from guarantors also.

15

Sick and Protested Advances Accounts

1. Sick Accounts

Sickness does not develop suddenly but it is a gradual process. There are number of factors which reflect tendency of units moving towards sickness. Some of the factors are:

(a) *Poor and unsatisfactory turnover in the account:* Poor and unsatisfactory turnover in the account can be due to decline in sales or diversion of sales proceeds through other channels.

(b) *Slow movement of stock:* Slow movement of stock shows that demand of material is declining and unit is likely to face financial problems.

(c) *Non-submission of stock statement:* Non-submission of stock statement is also an indicative of something wrong with the unit i.e. financial difficulties.

(d) *Valuation of stocks:* The units which are not doing well have a tendency to inflate valuation of stocks.

(e) *Large withdrawals:* Withdrawals in round figures or large amounts on cheques drawn in favour of parties, not connected with the business of the borrower, are also indicative of something being wrong with unit's position.

(f) *No drawing/tendering of bills, deposit bills etc:* No drawing/ tendering of bills, deposit bills etc. limits having sanctioned also shows that there has been little sales or no sales.

(g) *Frequent and large returning of bills:* Frequent and large returning of bills also indicate sickness of the unit.

(h) *Non-payment or delay in payment to labour and Govt. dues:* Non-payment or delay in payment to labour and Govt. dues also indicate sickness of the unit.

(i) *Non-payment of instalments under term-loans:* Non-payment of instalments under term loans also attracts attention towards sickness of the unit.

(j) *Frequent requests for excess drawings:* Frequent requests for drawings beyond sanctioned limit/ drawing power also indicate sickness of business enterprise.

(k) Violation of terms and conditions and non-submission of renewal proposals.

(l) Shortage of margin.

(m) Issuance of post-dated cheques and accommodation bills.

(n) Working results, financial position and analysis of Profit and Loss a/c, Balance Sheet etc. always indicate/tell whether a unit is doing well or not. Decline in production and sales are also an indicator of sickness, where other units in the same industry are doing well.

After proper analysis of causes of sickness proper steps should be taken to safeguard bank's interest. It is believed that the, unit has become sick and the amount outstanding is doubtful of recovery, account should be transferred to Protested Advances Category after obtaining permission of Competent Authority.

2. Protested Advances

Protested advances are classified in three categories viz.:

(a) Suit filed accounts,

(b) Decreed accounts,

(c) Others.

Debits are not allowed after transfer to Protested Advances Category.

Purpose of transfer of account to protested category is that utmost vigilance in realization of bank's dues is exercised. The account should be transferred to P.A. Category if it is felt that account has become wholly or partly doubtful of recovery after obtaining permission from Competent Authority.

While transferring an account to PA Category uptodate interest should be debited in the existing account. All returned bills, purchased or discounted should also be debited to PA A/c. A separate account for each advance should be opened in the PA Register with full particulars and balance should be tallied periodically with the General Ledger. The PA Register should be maintained category wise of PA Accounts, under different heads viz. Suit Filed A/cs, Decreed A/cs and others which should also tally with Subsidiary General Ledger.

16

Management of Non-performing Assets (N.P.A.)

In a developing economy like India, Banks, particularly nationalised commercial banks and financial institutions have a very big role to play. Beginning from late sixties, in order to fulfill social responsibility banks have been financing uninterruptedly for development of resources in national priority areas like agriculture, small scale industries, transport and for development of infrastructural facilities at the grass root level. With this Banks credit portfolio has grown by leaps and bounds both in terms of amount and number of accounts.

However, frequent announcements by Govt. for waiver of loan/ interest and many other exogenous and indigenous factors have spoiled the atmosphere for recovery of these loans. Trends show that during the last two decades or so, recovery of loan has become a major problem for banking industry, which has resulted in high overdues in the total assets of the banks. As a result of this, banks are not in a position to recycle their funds, which in turn has contributed to erosion of their profitability and viability.

With the liberalisation of the Indian Economy during early nineties, the era of open competition and efficiency coupled with concept of profitability and commercial viability has begun. To ensure that the Indian Financial Sector achieves International Standards, the RBI, based on Narsimham Committee Recommendations, introduced Prudential Norms for capital adequacy, exposure norms to big borrowers and norms for income recognition, asset classification and provisioning under a time bound implementation programme.

The Reserve Bank of India introduced Prudential Accounting Standards for Banks in April 1992. The essence of new system is recognition of record of recovery as the basis for classification of advances. Thus, if interest/ installment of principal remains unpaid for specification no. of quarters i.e. two quarters at present, an advance would be classified as Non-performing Asset (NPA) and depending upon the period for which it remained as NPA, it had to be classified as sub-standard or doubtful asset. If an advance was considered by internal or external auditor or an inspecting officer of the RBI as likely to involve a total loss for the bank considered an advance, it had to be classified as loss asset. All other advances were considered as performing or standard asset of the bank. Banks were advised to recognise the potential treat for memory of an NPA and to make appropriate provision for the intensity and nature of the Non-performing Asset.

Due to the implementation of revised RBI prudential norms for classification of advance as above, banks had to make huge provisions for NPAs and interest was not allowed to be recognised as income on them. Further an interest recognised as income during the previous years on assets which have become NPAs in later years and which has remained unrecovered was also to be derecognised.

Performance of banks during the last 9-10 years show that in terms of percentage, NPAs of banks as a whole have come down from 24 per cent in 1993 to 15 per cent in 2002, although the quantum has remained around Rs. 40000-45000 crores as per different reports in this regard.

Reduction in percentage and near status quo or marginal increase in absolute terms raises several issues in respect of management of NPAs. For Instance, whether the reduction in percentage terms is on account of an increase in advance, or due to dilution of norms of RBI in this regard? Which component namely, actual recovery, actual up-gradation, compromise or technical write-off is responsible for percentage reduction in NPAs? It is not clear whether it is due to sanctioning of fresh credit limits to delinquent borrowers or it is due to incidence of NPAs in credit limits sanctioned to new clients, ignoring prudence in this regard.

The concept of go-go banking leading to manifold increase in credit has brought with it own evils. More and more borrowers are turning willful defaulters taking the benefit of mainly inherent deficiencies in our legal system and other internal factors. Like the state governments loan waiver schemes etc.

The other major factors for poor recovery and account turning to non-performing asset for the banks may be summarised as under:-

1. Improper execution of documents.
2. Lack of timely monitoring and follow-up, inadequate field staff and apathy towards recovery.
3. Security erosion by the borrowers.
4. Indecisiveness at various levels.
5. Willful defaulters and interference by external forces.
6. Practical difficulties in enforcing securities.
7. Cumbersome, time consuming and costly legal process.

In fact there is no substitute for proper and timely monitoring of borrower accounts. Periodical inspections and verification of stocks and securities, their proper monitoring and follow-up would enable the banks to identify early symptoms of doubtful and bad debts. If a borrower becomes a defaulter and his account is identified as NPA, bank can proceed in two ways; either to file a suit in the court of law for recovery of dues or to adopt non-legal remedies depending upon the circumstances of each case.

For filing a suit, the bank has to examine various factors such as legal expenses, value and validity/ enforceability of securities, chances of recovery, antecedents of the borrowers etc. The bank has also to see that it should not spend its good money in pursuit of bad money. However, under circumstances where a willful defaulter may not be inclined to renew the documents, legal action may become necessary.

Of late non-legal remedies like compromise, re-habilitation, and merge/ acquisitions are gaining popularity amongst the banks and they have realised that litigation will never come to an end unless it is brought to end by them-selves. However, with the establishment of Debt Recovery Tribunals (DRTs) in most of the states cases can be filed with them in respect of big borrowal accounts where default amount is more than Rs. 10 Lacs. The position tilts towards initiating legal action in cases where the borrower is willful defaulter and have sufficient means to cover bank's dues. Setting up of DRTs has given a better recourse to the bank for early and effective disposal of court cases, which were long pending with the civil courts, as the later had neither sufficient expertise, nor resources for disposing of the same.

Compromise

Normally it would be in order for the banks to resort to the practice of compromise under the following circumstances:

(a) Inadequacy/deterioration in quality of security.

(b) Forced sale of charged securities may affect market value.

(c) The borrower/guarantor is of meagre means.

(d) The bank has already provided for the same (provision already made).

(e) Time value of money.

(f) The staff accountability has been examined and decided.

(g) It may not be wise to incur further expenses in the expectation of recovery after a considerable long time.

(h) No write-off of principal amount is proposed.

(i) The bank can recycle the amount received as compromise amount, and

(j) Chances of recovery through DRTs are remote.

As banks are increasingly resorting to compromise settlements it is desirable that Banks' Board of Directors should evolve an appropriate and transparent policy in respect of compromise settlement. While framing the policy it is necessary to decide the minimum that is acceptable to the bank as compromise amount, particularly where the sums are large and securities are available, although enforcement may take time.

Rehabilitation

When a unit becomes sick, it fails to generate income, which tells upon the repaying capacity of the borrower, and the advance may become NPA. In the genuine cases (sick viable units) funds are infused by way of rehabilitation package of merits of the case, it can start generating income thereby improving the recovery position of the banks. Once sickness is established and banks decide to offer rehabilitation package or such package as approved by BIFR, the bank has to show sympathy, sacrifice and speed where default is not wilful. Rehabilitation requires additional input of funds in a company, which has gone sick. As such decision should be taken carefully and judiciously. It is advisable that half-hearted measures are not taken and adequate amount of funds provided so that unit may be rehabilitated in reality and is in a position to generate surplus for repayment of bank's dues.

Merger/Acquisition

This is a process under which a sick unit is merged with a healthy unit or sometimes a healthy unit acquires a sick unit. A part of the consideration paid to the sick unit (company) is to liquidate its dues to banks, wholly or partially.

The merger/acquisition is specially beneficial to the healthy unit, under Section 72A of the Income Tax Act, if it is allowed to carry forward and set off accumulated losses and unabsorbed depreciation of the sick unit, provided the merger is approved by BIFR/ Govt. of India in the public interest.

In case of merger the sick unit, i.e., NPA will get immediately converted into a performing asset because it will acquire the status of the healthy unit. In fact the sick unit will be wiped out from the books of the bank and the healthy unit will show increased outstanding under different accounting heads.

Lodging Claims with DI and CGC/ECGC

Needless to say all eligible claims with DI and CGC/ ECGC should be lodged in time and followed-up vigorously so that funds are received and recycled by the bank.

It is to be admitted that in present scenario NPAs are at the core of the financial problems of the banks and ceaseless efforts are required to improve the recovery rate. Similarly advances which are not NPAs but are at the threshold should be given special attention because otherwise these may become NPAs sooner than later. Banks have to constantly upgrade their credit evaluation skills and system in order to successfully manage their loan assets.

The position of non-performing assets of all public sector commercial banks for the years 2002, 2003 and 2004 as at 3lst, March is as follows:

S. No.	*Name of Bank*	*Net NPA (Rs. Crores)*		
		2002	*2003*	*2004*
(A)	**Nationalised Banks**			
1.	Allahabad Bank	1160	887	363
2.	Andhra Bank	237	206	120
3.	Bank of Baroda	1913	1700	1761
4.	Bank of India	2304	2286	2062
5.	Bank of Maharashtra	480	459	1378
6.	Canera Bank	1288	1454	1271
7.	Central Bank of India	1699	1563	250
8.	Corporation Bank	253	198	884
9.	Dena Bank	1227	997	383
10.	Indian Bank	904	755	578
11.	Indian Overseas Bank	958	912	Nil
12.	Oriental Bank of Commerce	454	225	577
13.	Punjab and Sind Bank	651	639	449
14.	Punjab National Bank	1810	1527	532
15.	Syndicate Bank	690	700	753
16.	UCO Bank	724	697	845
17.	Union Bank of India	1338	1253	299
18.	United Bank of India	542	406	100
19.	Vijaya Bank	373	206	288
	Total (A)	19005	17072	12893
(B)	**State Bank of India**	6810	6183	5442
(C)	**Associate Banks of SBI**			
1.	SBBJ	342	282	107
2.	State Bank of Hyderabad	417	315	77
3.	State Bank of Indore	153	138	Nil
4.	State Bank of Mysore	362	273	186
5.	State Bank of Patiala	255	161	Nil
6.	State Bank of Saurashtra	204	164	Nil
7.	State Bank of Travancore	425	280	154
	Total (C)	2158	1613	525
	Total (B & C)	8968	7796	5967
	Total (A, B & C)	27973	24868	18807

Source: The Indian Banker, Mar, 2006.

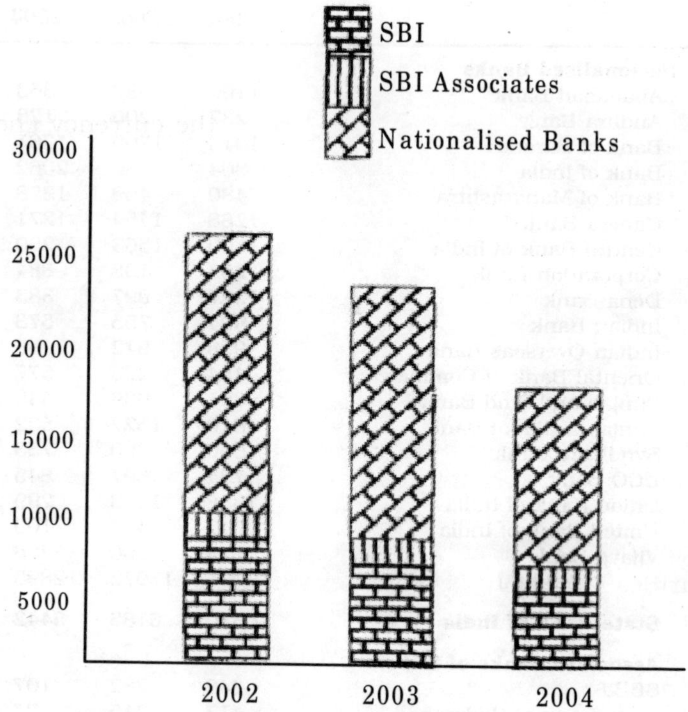

Source: IBA Bullentin, July 2004, p. 34.

17

Credit Risk Management

Commercial banks are custodian and trustee of money collected from public in the form of deposits. Surplus money available after meeting statutory requirements is deployed as advance to different sectors. Investment in shares and securities has also become prominent avenues for fund deployment. Incomes generated out of advance and investments assure growth and survival of a bank. Since advance is always associated with risks, any incorrect decision may block the fund and thus may fail to generate any income. Therefore, the decision in deployment of funds requires fair background of knowledge on how risks can be managed and minimised.

Any credit decision always demands proper evaluation and analysis of the proposal. Banks and financial institutions are already burdened with huge amount of non-performing assets (NPA), stronger the financial health of a bank. Every bank is striving hard to reduce the amount of NPA. Substantial reduction in percentage of net amount of NPA computed on total assets (advances) is a silent target for all banks. The way this target can be achieved is that on the one hand the amount of numerator should be reduced, on the other hand the quantum of advances is the amount of denominator should be increased.

Reduction of numerator needs curative as well as drastic steps depending upon merits because the amount consists of already identified NPA. The curative steps like nursing the accounts if found potentially viable and transferring them back to performing assets after one year of nursing period on being satisfied on regular recovery of instalments and interest as per rescheduled programme. The drastic steps may like gearing up recovery by continuous and vigorous follow-up or mutually agreeing for compromise by sealing down part of the dues offering some relief and concessions aiming at faster recovery of sticky dues on principle that a rupee recovered today. Writing off part of dues is also a mode of drastic steps taken where recovery prospect is found bleak.

The curative and drastic steps are the post mortem steps are required to be taken after the accounts have become NPA. The steps, therefore, should be taken sincerely as the banks should not remain idle leaving it to the mercy of the borrower to decide their time to repay at their choice. The other way of reducing percentage of NPA is to increase the amount of advances, which can be achieved by making additional advance as it increases the amount of denominator.

Banks cannot remain satisfied with old accounts only. They should mobilise new accounts and also improve advances by fresh lending and additional finance on merits. They should however remember not to be tempted to go on increasing advance in all sundry accounts as any fresh advance in wrong hands may add to the NPA.

Requirement of appropriate decision is most important in order to check any slippage of a performing asset into non-performing asset. It will have multiplied pressure as any fresh NPA will erode capital adequacy ratio on account of risk weight on the advance and at the same time no increase in profit as the account will stop providing any income.

The steps that should be required before an account is allowed to be NPA are the precautionary steps, which are most important to check any fresh NPA.

The process of credit risk management needs analysis of uncertainty, analysis of risk inherent in a credit proposal. The factors influencing the fate of a venture requires to be identified. Some risks are predictable whereas some may not be foreseen. The risks, which are predictable, can be minimised by formalising proper strategies whereas those, which are unpredictable, have to be faced and overcome.

Hence, any lending decision should always be preceded by detailed analysis of risks and outcome of the analysis should be taken as guide for credit decision.

The risks that normally are associated with a credit proposal can be broadly grouped into three heads:

- Industry risks.
- Management risks.
- Financial risks.

1. Industry Risks

Industry risks result from interruption in availability of those, which are physically required. They are the basic requirements for production. The others under the group of industry risk may appear at the postproduction stage i.e. in marketing of goods.

Industry risks may be present at the pre-marketing stage like interruption in availability of raw materials, labour, power, fuel, unfavourable government decisions viz. imposition of import duty on imported raw materials, unfavourable court verdict on pollution control measures forcing closure of the unit at advanced stage, increased bargaining power of supplier because of large number of options etc.

Industry risk at post - production stage may result from business cyclicality, globalisation, technological developments, quick rate of obsolescence, easy entry of strong multi-national companies, slow market growth than expected thus, resulting in poor turnover of stocks and increased bargaining power of buyers because of large number of options available etc.

2. Management Risks

Management of a concern or trading unit would mean the team of promoters/directors/partners and the key operating functionaries.

The management risks may appear due to adversity in integrity, track record, expertise, competence, commitment, capital market perception, confidence, patience, frankness, creativity, maturity of those functioning in management role etc.

3. Financial Risks

Financial risks are those that may result in adverse change in financial position compared to what was anticipated. The industry risks and management risks either singly or collectively may affect financial position of a concern or a trading unit.

Financial risks are measured and are considered present if the ratios like Current Ratio, Debt-Equity Ratio, Ratio of TOL to Equity, Profitability Ratio, Debtors and Creditors Turnover Ratios, Debt Service Coverage Ratio, IRR compared to average cost of capital are found unfavourable.

All the risks discussed above may or may not be present in all cases. Their intensity also may not be equal. While evaluating a credit proposal the foreseeable risks should be analysed. It will be too much optimism to expect all credit proposal to be free from risks, may be that a single risk will spoil the whole venture whereas despite presence of some risks the project would be viable on account of the other favourable factors. Hence, along with individual analysis of the element of each risk, the fate of a proposal should be considered in totality.

18

Security of Banks and Cash Management

The number of thefts/robberies in banks is on increase in present times, which requires us to study the importance of security of banks and cash management. Security of banks is of utmost importance as the commercial banks deals with hard cash, security arrangements are needed at all levels.

(A) Branch Premises/Location

(1) It should be ensured that the site selected for branch provides natural security i.e. it is not isolated or located in a crime prone area.

(2) The crime-proneness or vulnerability must be assessed before opening a branch. For this purpose the local police must be consulted and their comments taken into account.

(3) In selecting the site, a place as near to police station booth as possible, should be selected. If there is no police station/booth especially in rural areas then the place selected should be near a market place or any other public place such as near to post office, courts, hospital, school, college, railway station and bus stand etc.

(4) If the branch is located in market area the day on which the branch remains closed should preferably the same as the day on which the market is closed.

(5) In designing and constructing the building the strength of the material used for construction as well as the other static safeguard should be borne in mind.

(6) It should be ensured that the building is structurally safe from hazards of fire and theft.

(7) The premise selected should have high compound walls and there should be at least two entrances.

(8) It is necessary that the outer door have collapsible shutter in addition to the normal door. Similarly, the windows and the ventilators on outer walls should be provided with grills.

(9) It would be preferable to have the Branch Manager residence in the same premises.

(B) Branch Layout

(1) Standard layout for different classes of branches depending upon the size of the volume of business etc. should be worked out assuring functional efficiency as well as security requirements.

(2) As far as possible all departments should be on one floor only.

(3) The cash counter should be located as far away from the main entrance and as near the strong room/ cash safe as possible.

(4) The cash counter should be constructed keeping in view the security specifications.

(5) The layout should assure regulating customer traffic. Customer aisles should not pass through work areas, especially when cash is handled.

(6) In larger metropolitan or urban branches at least one work station having an overview of both the Branch Manager's cabin and the cash counters and if possible

the entrance to the strong room also, should be constructed.

(7) Cash Cabin's unit be enclosed by see-through partition walls. Thick plate glass or wire netting of 5 cm square may be used for the purpose. It must be ensured that registers and other books/ records are not piled against the partition thereby obstructing the view.

(8) The doors to the cash counters must be fitted with night latches so that once shut from within; they cannot be opened from outside operating the key.

(9) The Cashiers cabin should have a small windows at the near so that cheques, registers etc. can be passed through it without opening the door.

(10) The windows of all cash counters should be provided with sliding flaps which cannot be opened from outside.

(11) The height of the cash cage would be adequate to prevent a person standing outside from reaching the counter level.

(12) The breadth of the worktable on the cashier's side of the counter should likewise be such that, a person standing outside cannot reach the cash drawer level.

(13) The cash counter should have worktables at two levels one of the same level as the counter one for the customers and the second at a lower level where drawers for keeping cash will be fitted.

(14) The cash drawers should have proper locking arrangements.

(15) The cash window should provide space just enough for a hand to pass through.

(16) It should be ensured that there is adequate illumination during banking hours as also at night.

(17) Emergency lights should be provided at all necessary points.

(18) It should be ensured that fire-fighting equipment is sufficient for the branch and it is duly refilled so that the same should work at the time of need.

(19) There should be an independent source of power to the currency chest/ strong room.

(C) Other Safeguard

(1) Security alarm system is in perfect working condition, which should be periodically checked and serviced.

(2) Collapsible gate at the entrance of the branch should have a chain so that movement of customer is checked.

(3) Guards are being asked to stand in the branch at a place where they can be effective at the time of need.

(4) Gun license should be renewed on due date.

(5) Excess cash if any should immediately be removed to currency chest/sub-chest.

(6) The amount of cash sent from one point to another should not exceed the limit for which the transit insurance cover has been arranged.

(7) Security Officers should regularly visit branches and should display prominent telephone numbers of police station/fire brigade, etc., in the branch premises.

(8) The amount of cash at counter should not exceed the amount required as prescribed by the bank.

(9) The cash safe should be secured each time after it is opened.

(10) The main door of the branch should be closed and bolted from inside when cash is taken out of the strong room to the counters in the cash department and vice-versa. Where the arm-guard is available, he should escort such cash in transit.

(11) Dual control of Branch Manager and Cashier Incharge must be exercised invariably at all times.

(12) Cash must be taken out of the strong room/ cash safe on a minimum number of occasions.

(13) Where cash-van facility is available it is safer and advisable to avail the facility from link/ currency chest office to safeguard bank's interest.

(14) Proper secrecy must be observed at every point in case of inward/ outward movement of cash to protect bank's interest from anti-social elements. Secrecy includes secrecy of time, amount, identification of cashiers' staff, mode of transport and vehicle to be used etc.

(15) Individual bank must strictly follow the instructions of its HO/ZO/RM's office regarding cash management i.e. cash in hand should be kept at the minimum level as far as possible overnight each day to save H.O. interest and to protect the bank from loss of any mishappening which may occur overnight/ during business hours. Excess cash should be deposited in currency chest office of the bank or SBBJ/ SBI/ or any other bank's branch on regular basis.

(16) CCTV cameras should be installed wherever necessary for security arrangements in bank premises.

19

Preventive Measures to Avoid Frauds in Banks

Once upon a time when banks were quoted for honesty. But now a days for a banker, who deals in money, fraud is a normal occupational hazard, as it happens in the case of lathe machine (with which he works) is a normal occupational hazard despite this, if injury occurs it is painful.

Fear of accountability for some fraud or other among the employees is now very high. Earlier fear used to disappear on receipt of terminal benefits on retirement. The present position is such that fear not only runs all through the career, but also even after retirement. Pension can be stopped for the past mis-deeds also on discovery of latter one.

Let us first see what is fraud. Fraud is not defined in criminal law, yet it is commonly understood that it contains an element of cheating or an intention to cheat or deceive.

According to one survey 59 per cent of bank frauds have occurred with the connivance or collusion of employees. Still the redeeming feature is that majority of employees are honest. Staff involved in frauds compared to total strength may not even be one per cent. All category of staff irrespective of the cadre, are involved in frauds. No bank, whether private sector, public sector or foreign bank is an exception to these kind of occurrences.

People who commit frauds may be classified in these three major categories:

(1) Employees.

(2) Outsiders include customers, friends and relatives of employees and other anti-social elements of society.

(3) Collusion between employees and outsiders.

The most vulnerable aspects for frauds in banks are:

(a) New SB/CD accounts and

(b) Issuance of cheques books.

But it does not mean that other areas are not prone to frauds. Frauds have occurred in other areas also. However, major losses have occurred with repetition in the above-mentioned two areas only.

Other fraud-prone areas are:

(a) Several forged or fake DDs both inland and foreign have been encashed through new accounts opened in various banks.

(b) Several interest and dividend warrants have been intercepted in transit and have been encashed through fraudulently opened new SB accounts.

(c) Even FCNR and NRE accounts have been opened using fake passports.

(d) There are instances of foreign students who have managed to open new accounts with fictitious addresses with banks. Such accounts have been used to defraud banks by foreign DDs. Sizeable foreign exchange have been siphoned off, for alleged OGL fictitious imports by means of remittances through new opened current accounts, though in such fictitious payments, banks have not lost any money, the country lost valuable foreign exchange for nothing. New account holders in several instances managed to get loans against fake NSCs/KVPs/Title Deeds etc. and finally when the frauds were discovered, the account holders become untraceable as all addresses turned out to be bogus.

Thus, any numbers of domestic and foreign currency banking transactions could be quoted, where the banks have lost several crores of rupees due to negligence in opening new accounts.

Thus, it is evident that a chain of negligence starting with negligence in opening an account coupled with one or more negligence in the areas like issuance of cheques books, monitoring the account properly, reconciling inter-branch transactions etc. have enabled the perpetrators of fraud to carry out their operations successfully in banks. In addition to it there are other unfair means also, by which employees of banks (irrespective of cadre) are found committing frauds.

(e) By purchasing/ discounting bill/MTR/ RRs etc. that were found bogus and banks suffered heavy losses.

(f) By manipulating accounts passing wrong vouchers and crediting his account, specially in provision vouchers of interest on deposits.

(g) By receiving money in loan accounts and not depositing in related account deliberately.

(h) By receiving money in deposit accounts viz. RD, SB account and not crediting in related account for a long time satisfying customers by making entries in the pass-books uptodate.

(i) By putting forged currency notes in cash of bank at the time of opening cash and drawing original currency notes in exchange specially in currency-chest branches where huge Government money lies with banks which is checked occasionally.

Main Reasons of Frauds

- As pointed out earlier one reason, i.e., negligence, in observing the well laid down norms.
- Second reason may be decline in moral values and attitudes of employees over period of time.
- Third may be adverse family circumstances, burdensome expenditure on chronic sickness and marriage of family members under which one may be forced to adopt unfair means.

Precautions Necessary for Avoiding Frauds in Banks

As pointed out earlier necessary precautions should be observed while opening new SB/RD accounts which are as under:

- By obtaining photographs of the account-holder.
- Proper introduction of person known to bank or account-holder.
- By sending letter of thanks to the introducer.
- Formal and informal enquiries with the proposed customer.
- Monitoring the transactions, particularly high value credits for at least six months.
- Subjecting high value instruments to ultra violet/ ultra red machine.
- Due care should be observed while issuing cheque books to newly opened account-holder asking his need and occupation to safeguard bank's interest.
- Proper enquiry should be made if a new account is opened to collect instruments, which are dated prior to the date of opening of account.

Letter of thanks or SMS should be sent to new customers to check and confirm their address or mobile number.

Similarly given below are some of the laxity in the case of issuance of cheque books which have become a cause of frauds:

- Issuance of cheque books without insisting for cheque requisition slips, particularly of third parties against letters. Sometimes such letters are also either on plain paper or improper letterheads.
- Bad English/forged handwriting.
- Signature in the letter is also forged.

Under the circumstances mentioned above cheque books should be sent to by registered post instead of delivering it to the third party himself who brings the letter to avoid chances of fraud. Now-a-days some banks have adopted the procedure under which cheque book is sent to the customer by their controlling office by speed post on his/ her address to safeguard customers/ bank's interest against fraudulent use.

Periodical job rotation should be order of the day, no one is indispensable, and if any one is there it is better to be watchful.

Similarly, if a person in staff never takes leave also, it is a matter of enquiry if not investigation.

Suddenly if life-style of the employee changes it is better to enquire from which lottery he won the prize.

Similarly, when large credits suddenly starts pouring into any of the account which were operated for moderate amounts earlier it is better to enquire from the account-holder in a friendly way about the source of credits, in addition to ensuring that there is no laxity on our part.

To sum up, I would like to suggest that "be a defensive driver and follow the traffic signals seriously, chances in that case are limited". Think it over again, what is defensive driving and what are traffic signals (precautionary measures to avoid frauds) in Banking.

20

Precautionary Measures to Avoid Housing Loan Frauds in PSBs

The share of Housing Loan in retail banking operations of PSBs is the highest. The main reason for this is, that, housing loans offer maximum security, fixed yield, longer maturity period, opportunities to the Banks to cross sell other products and also its eligibility for coverage under priority sector credit. On the other hand, lower interest rate regime, income tax exemptions on accrued interest and repayment of instalments, Group Life Insurance product at a concessional rate to cover the loans outstanding in case of death, Free Personal Accident Insurance cover under group policy have made housing loans more attractive for growing Indian middle class. Longer gestation period, sentimental attachment for a dream Home and appreciation in value of house property in course of time are factors that leverage borrowers to serve housing loans easily without any difficulty. Easy documentation formalities, hassle free loan and cut throat competition amongst Banks have led to a significant and unprecedented growth of Housing Sector across the length and breadth of the country. However, this unparalleled growth is not without cost and not without effort, some weaknesses have emerged. Instances of frands and forgeries have perpetrated in Housing Loan segmest involving crores of rupees. While Banks draw comfort by way of security in housing loan segment, there are instances of multiple financing against fake title deeds and impersonation. The fabrication of income documents, balance sheets etc. are common modus operandi to defraud Banks. Other modus operandi is misuse of loan with connivance of Builders / Dealers. The preventive vigilance is an important tool to check such frand and forgeries as it treats the cause of disease rather than to treat the disease. The preventive vigilance helps the banks in creating the alertness foresightedness and a sense of responsibility among employees for observing systems and procedures.

Preventive Vigilance Action Points

In view of the growing trend of frauds in housing loan segment, an in-depth study of the types of frauds, modus operand of each case and their preventive measures are given as under:-

Sl. No.	*Types of fraud*	*Modus operandi*	*Suggestive preventive measures*
1.	Fabrication of income documents like income tax return, salary slip, Balance Sheet etc.	Committed generally by borrowers in connivance with builder/promoter / Estate Agent etc.	• Personal verification of original salary slips and attendance register with the employer. • Comparing salary amount with the bank statement. • Cross verification of balance sheet with bank statement. • Personal interview of borrower and visit to site.
2.	Other income of the proponents like agriculture, coaching, tuition income were accepted. Income of non working spouse purportedly running hobby classes, cooking classes, Tailoring classes, Beauty parlours, Mahandi classes,	Committed generally by well dressed, well educated hi-fi borrowers who utilize the services of common Chartered Accountants in fabricating income tax returns and other methodology.	• Agriculture income can only be considered fit is supported by land record and income is reported in income tax return though not taxed. • In case agricultural income is considered, instalment should coincide with harvesting of crop.

Sl. No.	*Types of fraud*	*Modus operandi*	*Suggestive preventive measures*
	Dance and yoga classes, Computer job work etc were clubbed to inflate loan amount.		• Status verification of business must be done before accepting proof of income from such business / profession.
3.	Loan amount disbursed by way of pay order/ Demand draft are encashed by 3rd party/agent.	Disbursed amount of pay order/ demand draft are collected by 3rd party/agent from the borrower's banks and deposited in fictitious account opened for this purpose and amounts are withdrawn from such bogus account.	• Pay order/ demand draft etc. should be issued in the name of bankers to the builders/ promoter wherever as the case may be with the bank account number mentioned on it. • One rubber stamp should be affixed on the reverse of demand draft/ pay order/ banker's cheque stating "collecting banker should exercise utmost caution while collecting this instrument specially in the case of newly opened account." • Pay order/DD/ banker's cheque etc. should not be handed over to the borrower/ agent / 3rd party. Bank's officials can be sent for delivery of the instrument to the builders/sellers of the property at the registered address mentioned in the title deeds.
4.	Title documents/ stamped documents being forged by borrower/ builder.	Colored Xerox copy of various documents are produced including encumbrance certificate, fake stamp paper etc.	• Tracking and sharing of information among banks about black listed builders. The Title deeds to be

Sl. No.	Types of fraud	Modus operandi	Suggestive preventive measures
		which are difficult to distinguish/ identify from the original one.	handed over to advocate by bank only and by all his queries should be routed through bank only. The fee will also be paid through bank. • Bank officers should verify genuineness and correctness of the documents independently through their own advocates/ solicitors. • Sub-registrar's office may be approached to verify the genuineness of the stamp paper documents/ registration receipts etc. in case of any doubt. • The title deeds may be exposed to ultra-violet rays to differentiate between original and fake title deeds agreements for sale. While genuine stamp paper will glow in presence of ultra-violet rays, fake one will not glow.
5.	Over valuation of the property	These frauds are committed to draw higher loan amount by the borrower in connivance with the builder/ valuers. The value of property is inflated by including various non-existing expenditures.	• In case of doubt, valuation reports may be closey scrutinized by making discreet enquiries about various costs indicated in the valuation report. • In case of valuation over Rs. 25 lacs, two independent valuers should do valuation.

Sl. No.	*Types of fraud*	*Modus operandi*	*Suggestive preventive measures*
			• Government should introduce certificate course for approved valuers • Bank should develop in house expertise for valuation of properties.
6.	Multiple Financeing	The miscreants with intent to play fraud on bank connived with the Chairman/ Secretaries of housing cooperative societies and borrowers, prepared a number of original sets of documents in respect of a single flat/ land and availed loans from several banks using those fake but apparently original sets of documents. In the process, the miscreants could, get the owner's clear and marketable title to the property certified from the lawyers and in turn creation of equitable mortgage by depositing title deeds.	• Tracking and sharing of information among banks and housing finance companies about black listed builders through market intelligence. • Relevant testimonials like Bye-Laws, Firm Registration certificate, colonizer license of builders should be verified carefully with appropriate issuing authority. • Banks should insist on original title deeds of the landed property on which structure is built for verification. • Banks should insist on registration of property before releasing 1st instalment of loan. However, in that case "provisional sanction letter" may be issued to the borrower in this borrower in this regard provided all other terms and conditions are being complied with.

Sl. No.	Types of fraud	Modus operandi	Suggestive preventive measures
			• In case of purchase of property from government agency/ other agency on their behalf/ cooperative society etc., allotment letter of such agency issued in favour of buyer should be obtained. • Agreement to sale and documents of title should be in demat form.
7.	Cancellation of booking of flats/ shops/ property etc.	In this instant case after availing the 1st instalment, of loan amount, the booking is cancelled is collusion with borrower and builder/ promoter and the borrower directly taking the refund from the builder/ promoter.	• Credit rating of builders by CRISIL should be mandatory. • Bank should check past track record, financial viability, project execution capacity, clear title deeds, customer satisfaction of previous projects and technical competence of the builders. • Registration receipt issued by registar of Assurances should bear hypothecation clause. • Bank should obtain tripartite agreement (Registered) with builder, bank and borrower stating that if booking is cancelled, the money will be refunded to bank only.

Sl. No.	*Types of fraud*	*Modus operandi*	*Suggestive preventive measures*
8.	Sale of property by loanee without clearing existing loan.	Property is sold through duplicate/fake title deeds even though the legal title is with the Bank.	• Internal due diligence plays important role to prevent this type of frauds. • Bank to represent to RBI and GOI to enact legislation for creation of Equitable Mortgage in the office of Registrar of Assurances. • Credit rating of builders/realtors should be stipulated as terms of sanction.
9.	Misrepresentation of end use of loan.	Loan taken for residential Housing property but commercial property is constructed.	• Bank's officer to verify end use of loan in addition to verification by architect/ engineer as per system.
10.	Sale of property by builder without clearing dues of financing bank/ financial institution.	Builders sold constructed houses but did not pay the dues of bank/ financial institutions raised for construction of the building.	• Construction/funding of loan should be closely supervised. • Original title deeds/ documents should be called for appraisal at the time of sanction of loan. • Bank to keep eyes on builder and seek information for sale of flat/ houses on regular basis. • Bank should obtain an affidavit from the builder stating that no financial assistance has bean received against the houses under construction and no plots/ flats are mortgaged in any bank/ financial institution.

Observance of KYC norms - as a Tool of Preventive Vigilance

RBI has reiterating the extent guidelines and instructions on KYC from time to time to prevent frauds. These guidelines pertains to identification of new customers - both individual and corporate, establishing identity of the customers by obtaining PAN card, driving license, voter identity card, pass-port, marriage certificate, address card, ration card, bank's pass book, water and electricity bills, telephone bill etc, conducting due diligence and reporting of such transactions, obtaining credit report of borrowers dealing with other banks before making advance/ taking over accounts. The RBI has recently reiterated following guidelines for strict compliance by the banks:

- To do customer identification before opening account either through introductory reference or through documents such as voter identity card, PAN card, pass-book, passport, driving license etc.
- To obtain photograph of the customers both in deposits and loan accounts.
- To verify all relevant facts provided by the borrower including income particulars, sources of income, property to be purchased, land on which construction is to be done, repaying capacity, reputation/standing of applicant etc.
- To record cash transactions both deposit and withdrawal of Rs. 10 lacs and above in a separate register and to report such transactions including any other suspicious transactions to respective controlling offices.
- To obtain PAN for issuance of travellers cheques, NEFT, demand drafts, mail transfers and telegraphic transfers etc of rupees above Rs. 50000/-. In case of deposit in SB/CA accounts and Loan accounts Rs. 50000/- and above PAN is also obtained by banks.

- To insure compliance of Foreign Contribution Regulation Act 1976 while opening accounts or collecting cheques by insisting to account holder to furnish certificate of registration with the Govt. of India (GOI)
- To train and educate staff for anti-money laundering guidelines and implementing KYC policies consistently.
- To ask concurrent auditors/ internal inspector to check and report compliance of KYC norms.

The above discussion on prevention of frauds for housing loan by PSBs is not exhaustive; the miscreants may discover other methods to commit frauds in future.

21

Preventive Measures to Avoid Frauds of ATMs in PSBs

Automatic Teller Machine is an electronic machines, which is linked to accounts and records of a banking institution. It enables customers to carry out banking transactions without visiting bank premises. The need to visit bank premises for cash withdrawal or for depositing cheques/instruments is no more necessary as these transactions can be undertaken through Automatic Teller Machines (ATMs) which are installed at different prominent and convenient locations by banks. Millions of ATM transactions are successfully carried out every day around the globe. The technology has made it possible for a customer to transact business on line, any time from any location It is also possible to use ATMs installed by other banks under arrangement.

ATMs are virtual banks, which allows the user to withdraw cash, pay bills, balance inquiries, cash deposits etc. The machine is operated with the help of on access device, which is card, code (Personal Identification Number), or through other means of access to a customer's account, or any combination thereof. Some ATMs are also debit cards, which can be used for making purchases. Customers' account is charged immediately on purchases.

Frauds relating to Automatic Teller Machines may be committed both by outsiders and insiders. It is understandable that as the number of transactions rise, the number of fraud occurrences will also rise. However, it is not proper to say that ATMs have become more susceptible to fraud.

Frauds can occur due to negligence on the part of the card holder or due to lack of altertness on the part of the bank. If the card holder does not follow the common precautionary measures as mentioned below, he is exposed to risk.

Frauds may occur in the following ways:

(1) A cheat may go through the discarded receipts or carbons to illegally find out the card number.

(2) A dishonest clerk makes an extra imprint from credit card or charge card for his/her personal use.

(3) Card holder may receive a post card or letter or telephone call advising that he has been selected by computer through random draw for a free trip or bargain priced travel package or a costly gift at a throw away price. For availing the advantage of the gift under the lucky draw, the card holder has to contact at a particular telephone number. He is asked to furnish credit card number for becoming member of the resort so that he can be billed for the membership fee, or for token price of the gift which is being offered at a throw away price. However, instead of getting the product or services promised the account gets debited.

Precautionary Safeguards for Customers

Common sense is the best guide to use ATM safely. While using an ATM you should know the following:

(a) Relating to PIN and Card

(1) Protect the secrecy of your Personal Identification Number (PIN). Protect your ATM Card as you protect hard cash.

(2) Do not keep your bank ATM card and PIN together. Do not write PIN on the card or at a place where it can be discovered

(3) Do not give information regarding your ATM Card or PIN over the telephone to anyone even one claiming to be from your bank. Criminals who fraudulently use cards for telephone and online transactions do not have to give a PIN or signature to the merchant on the phone or online. The charges are simply debited directly to your account. You would not come to know until you get your next bank statement.

(4) Neither lend your ATM card to anyone nor reveal PIN to another person. Doing this may tempt that person to conduct transactions using the PIN or Card.

(5) Before disposing old cards, cut them up through the account number.

(6) Carry only those cards that you anticipate you will need.

(7) Sign your new cards as soon as you receive them.

(8) Keep a record of your card numbers, their expiration dates, and the phone number and address of each bank in a secure place.

(9) For protection of ATM and debit cards that involve a PIN, keep your PIN a secret. Do not use your birth date, phone number, house numbers as the PIN.

(10) Do memorise the PIN.

(11) Change your ATM PIN at least once in every two months.

(12) The best protections against card fraud are to know where your cards are at all times to keep them secure.

(b) Relating to withdrawals

(1) Remember not to leave your Card at the ATM.

(2) Never allow yourself to be distracted while carrying out your transaction.

(3) Don't accept assistance from anyone you do not know when using an ATM.

(4) Do not display your cash, pocket it as soon as the ATM transaction is completed and count the cash later when you are in safety of your own car, home or other secure surrounding.

(c) Relating to ATM

(1) If you are using an ATM that requires your card to open the door, do not permit an unknown person to enter with you. Once inside the vestibule, make sure the door is completely closed behind you.

(2) Choose an ATM that is well lighted and monitored by a surveillance camera or a security guard.

(3) Minimise your time at the ATM. Have your card ready. If you are making a deposit fill up pay-in-slip (deposit slip) at home, seal the envelope before you reach the ATM.

(4) Use your free hand to cover the ATM keyboard while you type in your PIN. Prevent others from seeing you enter your PIN by using your body to shield their view.

(5) Do not re-enter your PIN if the ATM swallows your card. Contact the bank immediately.

(6) Use an ATM only where and when you feel completely comfortable.

(7) Pay attention to the machine before using it. If something appears unusual or unfamiliar, use another ATM.

(8) Never use an ATM, which looks suspicious.

(9) Never use ATMs that have messages or signs fixed to them indicating that the sereen directions have been changed, specially if the message is posted over the card reader.

(10) Do not insert your ATM card into an obscurely placed ATM machine, or one with a card slot protruding from the face of the machine.

(d) Relating to surroundings

(1) When you make a transaction, be aware of your surroundings. Before proceeding with your transaction, look around to guard against surveillance by anyone who may arouse your slightest suspicion.

(2) If you suspect something is not quite right, trust your instincts. Use an ATM or a bank branch where your feel more comfortable. If possible, use a machine that is located in a bank location. It may be easier for criminal to tamper with a machine that is in a non-bank location.

(3) Report immediately any suspicious activity or crimes to both the bank and police.

(4) If you see anything suspicious, immediately cancel your transaction and leave. As soon as possible confirm with your bank that the transaction was indeed cancelled.

(5) At a drive-up ATM, keep your engine running, lock all of your doors, and close all windows except your own.

(6) When using an indoor ATM, be sure to lock your Car/ scooter etc. and take your keys with you, do not ever leave your car/scooter etc. running.

(7) Look out for suspicious activity or if there are suspicious looking individuals in the vicinity near the ATM particularly if it is after sunset. At night, be sure that the facility (including the parking area and walk-ways), is well lighted. Consider having someone accompany you when you use the facility, especially after sunset. If you observe any problem, go to another ATM.

(8) If you notice anything suspicious or if any other problem arises after you have begun an ATM transaction, you may want to cancel the transaction, pocket your card and leave. You might consider using another ATM or coming back later.

(e) Relating to Loss (theft of card)

(1) Report the loss, theft or unauthorized use of card or PIN to Bank without any loss of time. A stolen ATM/ Debit Card can be taken to any merchant and used to charge purchases to your "account". All that is needed is a forged signature. This can drain your account.

(2) Once you discover the theft you must report it to the police, close your account, open a new one and get new bank card.

(3) If you find electronic banking transaction is incorrectly reported on a receipt or statement, promptly notify Bank of the loss, Theft or unauthorised use of card or PIN will keep you exposed to risks.

(4) If you notice transactions you did not make, or if your balance has dropped suddenly without activity by you, immediately report the problem to your Bank. Some one may have co-opted your account information to commit fraud. Use the special telephone number that many card issuers list on their billing statements. Do not forget to follow up your phone call with a letter.

(f) Relating to Other Miscellaneous Activities

(1) Always request a receipt for your transaction. Compare your record with the account statements you receive. Mark each transaction in the statement of account, but not while at the ATM.

(2) Always save your ATM receipts. Do not leave them at the ATM because they may contain important account information.

(3) Carefully check ATM or debit card transactions before you enter the PIN or sign the receipt; the frauds for this item will be fairly quickly transferred out of your account to other account.

(4) Do not sign a blank charge or debit slip. Draw a line through blank spaces on charge or debit slips above

the total when you sign card receipts so the amount can not be changed.

(5) Tear up carbons and save your receipts to check against your monthly statements.

(6) Ensure the card is swiped in your presence.

For Bankers

Many banks have outsourced maintenance and cash replenishment services for ATMs. Though the outsourcing has been done to concerns of repute, still the chances of banks suffering losses can not be completely eliminated as human element is involved and one can not predict what undergoes in one's mind. Bankers have, therefore, to be very vigilant at each and every stage. It is not the reputation of the firm but the intention of its employee that matters.

(a) Relating to Cash Replenishment in ATM: The staff of the agency that has been awarded cash Replenishment contract in ATMs opens the machines, removes the cassette (bin) containing left over cash and replaces it with cassette (bin) filled with currency notes. The bank reimburses the service provider as per the contract.

(1) At the time of removal of cassettee (bin), if the bank officials do not verify the left over cash, there is a probability of over-billing the amount by the agency.

(2) The bank has to call for details of residue cash in each ATM on a day to day basis and has also to do surprise verification by counting residue cash. If this procedure is not adhered to then the bank is exposed to financial risk.

(3) The bank has also to find out the amount of cash withdrawn from each ATM and whether the amount withdrawn and the residue amount in the bin tallies with the amount fed by the agency.

(4) Bank should understand that the cash in ATM is cash in hand hence it should be physically verified at regular intervals.

(b) Relating to Internal Control Mechanism: Poor control by the bank over unused cards, PINs, returned mail, credit limit increase and changes in addresses can contribute to credit card and ATM card frauds. Delay in payments to merchants and payments from card holders could signal the beginning of problems with a third party service (generally an outside marketing agency).

(1) Separate the duties between the card issuing function and issuance of PIN.

(2) Have proper control of unissued cards and PIN. Have periodical verification.

(3) Act promptly on returned mail and customer complaints.

(4) Have proper control of credit limit increase.

(5) Change in address should be recorded without any delay and confirmation to be sent.

(6) Ensure that there are no unusual delays in receipt of cards and PINs by the customers.

(7) Ensure that payment authorization system functions correctly and there is no frequent malfunction is reported.

(8) Follow "know your customer norms" and do not open credit card merchant accounts without obtaining any background information on the merchant.

(9) Be careful, if credit card merchant account activity reflects an increase in the number and size of charge slips. Merchant has a sudden or unexplained increase in the level of authorization requests from a particular merchant location.

(10) Credit card merchant account deposits appear to exceed the level of customer activity observed at the merchant's place of business.

(11) Keep a track to find out if member establishment is depositing sales drafts made payable to a business or businesses other than the business named on the account.

(12) Have a watch on the account, if member establishment frequently requests telegraphic transfer of funds from the account to other institutions in other parts of the country or to almost immediately after deposits are made.

(13) Merchant is engaged in telemarketing activities and is the subject of frequent customer complaints.

(14) Though the member establishment has access to EDC (Electronic Data Capture) equipment but frequently inputs creditcard account numbers manually.

Action Points for Banks to Safeguard itself from Risk

(1) How many persons use ATM at a particular location?

(2) Whether the amount withdrawn meets replenishment?

(3) Is there sudden spurt in withdrawals from an ATM at a particular location?

(4) Whether cash is withdrawn frequently through an ATM card from different locations?

(5) What is the average daily withdrawal from a particular ATM?

(6) Whether frequent complaints pertaining to insufficient cash are received in respect of an ATM located at a particular place?

(7) Whether every day the one particular person replenishes cash in the bins of ATM and removes the bin containing residue cash?

(8) Whether Non-ATM Card holders visit the place immediately after the ATM was operated by an individual?

(9) Review customer complaints, no matter how significant they appear to be.

(10) Be sure proper controls are in place at all points throughout the card issuing and transaction processing functions.

(11) Review possible causes of frequent malfunctions of the payment authorisation system and follow up on remedial actions taken by the institution.

(12) Conduct on site inspections of merchant's operations.

(13) Monitor the traffic at ATM.

Points about ATM Crimes

E-mail and internet-related fraud schemes are being perpetrated with increasing frequency, creativity, and intensity with the help of latest technology, fraudsters dupe innocent consumers through, ATM and Internet. Knowing the latest trends in the scamming can protecting from being duped. While it is difficult to guarantee protecting from ATM scammers, there are security tips that lessen the risk. Never use suspicious looking ATM or odd-looking equipment or wires. Always monitor your accounts regularly to make sure that there is no unusual entry in the account. Although there is no conclusive evidence on the precise methods used in the suspected fraudulent cases reported so far, it is suspected that at least some involve tampering with ATMs. A few of the methods adopted by the fraudsters are quoted below:

Phishing

Phishing in the center stage in internet scams. It is the practice of sending e-mails at random, purporting to come from a genuine company operating on the Internet. In an attempt to trick customers fraudsters' request disclosing information at a bogus website operated by them. In their e-mails fraudsters usually claim that it is necessary to 'update' or 'verify' the password and they urge you to click on a link from the e-mail that takes you to the bogus website. Any information entered on the bogus website in captured by the criminals for their own fraudulent purposes. The scammer gets your username and password once you log into a banking website. A key logger then records your information and takes screen shots of your P.C. activity. ATM phishing is possible when particulars of card and PIN are divulged over internet, this enables cheats to produce counterfeit cards for fraudulent ATM cash withdrawals.

It is said by Experts that phishing scams can be prevented if you install a fire wall or frequently run and update anti-virus software and do not divulge PIN, card number and the name of issuing institution.

While phishing remains a high concern, experts also caution consumers against high-risk internet use. Experts advise consumers to monitor their accounts regularly. Always be aware of e-mails asking you to click on a link or confirm your details. If in doubt, phone the organisation first. Visit your credit card issuer's website for their latest advice on secure online shopping with a password.

Skimming

Those scammers, who target ATM users, use the latest technology to their advantage. *Fraud-sters* make counterfeit ATM cards by using a skimmer, which is a card-swipe device that reads the information on a consumer's ATM card. Scammers insert onto an ATM, ready to swipe information from unsuspecting customers. They take a blank card and encode all information from an ATM card when they swipe. The skimmer catches the PIN through a small camera mounted on the ATM. The consumer is unaware that without even the card has been stolen they have been scammed. Therefore, watch out for unusual devices on ATM machines as cards can be skimmed and reproduced.

The "Labanese Loop"

Scammers insert a portable steel loop into an ATM card slot. The scammer usually approaches the victim while at the machine, and poses as the person next in line. Victims are advised to enter their PINs three times and then hit cancel to get the machine to accept the cards. The scammer is able to memorise the PIN for future use and the machine keeps the card because of excessive number of attempts to enter the correct PIN. Victims leave in frustration because they could not get any money and they have lost their card. Once the loop is taken out of the ATM the scammer has the card and the PIN number for future transactions. This is relatively new scam that many experts believe will be short-lived due to fast technology upgrades.

Pretexting

This scam involves getting your personal information under false pretenses. For example, some one contacts you claiming to be from the security department of your bank. They ask you to verify personal information over the phone, such as your birth date, or your mother's maiden name. Sometimes the caller may even know a piece of personal information about you that may help to convince you that they are a legitimate bank representative.

The pretext caller then sell your personal information to people who may use it to get credit in your name. Do not, under any circumstances, give your any personal or banking information out over the phone, especially if you do not initiate the phone call.

Be discriminating when providing personal information online. Never give your personal or account information to any-one you do not trust. Make sure you verify business legitimacy by visiting its website. Ask the caller to give his phone number to enable you to respond. Immediately contact bank and inform.

Spoofing

In a "spoofing attack", the attacker creates a misleading context to trick you into making an inappropriate security-relevant decision. For example, criminals have set up bogus automated teller machines, typically in public areas or shopping malls. The machines would accept ATM cards and ask for PIN codes. Once the machine has the PIN, criminals have enough information to steal from the account.

In the end, ATM frauds not only cause financial losses, but may also hamper customer's confidence in using ATMs, which would run counter the industry's efforts in encouraging greater use of electronic channels of delivery. It is, therefore, in the interest of banks to prevent ATM frauds. The nature and extent of precautionary measures to be adopted will, however, depend upon the requirements of respective banks.

To conclude, ATM fraud is not the sole problem of banks alone, it is a big threat, which requires a coordinated and cooperative action on the part of the bank, customers and the law enforcement machinery.

PART – III

22

Profitability in Banks - Need and Measures

Many changes have taken place in banking industry, which have created an urgency to establish a system of profit budgeting. The impending transparency in accounts has all the more necessitated that banks should have high profit if they have to survive. Profitability has become most important parameter for judging the performance of a bank. RBIs income recognition; asset classification, provisioning, capital adequacy and NPA norms have far-reaching effect on profitability of banks.

All of us know, profit is a paramount necessity of any business organisation to survive. Profit is surplus of income over expenditure. Profitability is the earning capacity of a bank branch in relation to its funds. The income and expenditure of a bank branch comprise of the following components:

Income	*Expenditure*
1. Interest and Discount received.	1. Interest paid on deposits.
2. Commission, exchange and Guarantee fee.	2. Establishment expenses.
	3. Rent, taxes, insurance etc.
3. Interest allowed by H.O.	4. Postage, telegrams, stamps etc.
4. Rent including locker rent	5. Depreciation.
5. Miscellaneous incomes	6. Interest charged by H.O.
	7. Other expenses.

Spread: Interest earned on advances minus interest paid on deposits.

Burden: Non-interest expenses minus (–) Non-interest income.

Profit: Spread is more than burden.

Loss: Burden is more than spread.

Spread depends on the quantum of deposits and credit and deposit-credit mix and can be improved by taking funds (deposits) at low rate of interest and deploying funds (credit) at higher rate of interest.

Burden depends on quantum of non-interest income and expenditure. This can be improved by securing more:

- Non-fund business.
- Ancillary business.
- Recoveries of establishment expenses from borrowers.
- By minimising expenditure on T.A. Bills, stationery, electricity, telephone, water etc.
- Avoiding wasteful expenditure, adequate and proper use of manpower i.e. Staff.

Action Points

(1) *Cash Management*

(a) Cash in hand be kept minimum, it should always be below 1 per cent.

(b) Excess cash is remitted invariably.

(c) Branches having currency chest must transfer cash every Friday after keeping nominal cash.

(2) *Interest allowed by HO*

(a) BM to ensure that correct interest is being allowed by HO at prevailing rate of interest.

(b) Interest is paid on HO balance and remittance in transit account.

(c) Interest is paid for small and medium branches on

2nd week's of balance of previous month for large branches an average of balance of all the weeks of previous month.

(3) *Interest Charged by HO*

BM to ensure that correct interest is charged @ 12 per cent p.a. for metropolitan and urban branches and @ 11 per cent p.a. for semi-urban/ rural branches.

(4) *Provisioning of Interest*

BM to ensure that correct provision is being provided on deposits and advances.

(5) *Locker Rent*

BM to ensure that locker rent is being recovered as per rules and no locker is vacant. Locker, which is not in operation for a long period, should also be scrutinised and notices should be sent to its holders.

(6) *Managing NPA*

(a) BM to ensure recovery of derecognised interest.
(b) BM to ensure that there is no slippage of existing standard accounts to NPA.
(c) BM to hold immediate dialogue with borrowers where accounts are already under NPA and recovery of over dues and interest must be maximised.
(d) Possibility of early recovery by way of compromise proposal be explored.
(e) All eligible cases are filed under RACO Act for recovery and close liaison be kept with Revenue Authorities.

(7) *Subsidies*

BM to ensure that the following subsidies are claimed and received in time:

(a) *DRI:* 8½ per cent on outstanding balance as on last Friday of each month.

(b) *NRE:* 2 per cent on term deposits.

(c) *NABARD:* 3 per cent on balance outstanding on last Friday of each month.

(d) *Priority Sector:* 2½ per cent p.a. on advances under weaker sector excluding DRI and direct agriculture advances to small and marginal farmers included in weaker sector.

(8) *Refinance*

BM to ensure that refinance is being claimed and received timely from NABARD, SIDBI, Khadi Board and other Government Agencies like DRDA.

(9) *Deposit/Credit Mix*

BM to ensure that whether present deposit/ credit mix is proper and profitable. Current and saving deposits should be encouraged and brought to the level of 15 per cent and 25 per cent of total deposits.

(10) *Interest on Advances*

BM to ensure that interest including penal interest and commitment charges are being charged. A sample check is to be done on big borrowers, accounts.

(11) *Suspense*

(a) Outstanding in Suspense A/c be kept at minimum level.

(b) BM to ensure that reimbursement of suspense pension and other items are claimed and received within minimum possible time.

(12) *ODD*

Outstanding under ODD be kept at minimum level, as it is not yielding any income.

(13) *Service Charges*

BM to ensure that Incidental Charges, processing fee, GK's. Salary, Conveyance, Cheque-book charges, cheque-returning charges, duplicate pass-book charges, draft commission, locker operation charges etc. are being recovered accurately.

(14) *Expenditure*

(a) Ensure that all expenses incurred are for genuine reason and appropriate.

(b) Expenses on telephone, conveyance, stationery, TA bills, postage, water, electricity etc. are reasonable and under control. These expenses should commensurate with the business of bank's branch office. Moreover it is a check on losses. As all of us know a check on expenses enables a unit to earn more profit.

(c) Adequate and skilled man-power:

Surplus staff, if any, may be avoided or deputed elsewhere.

(15) *Follow-up of Draft-payable Entries*

Draft payable imprest entries should be monitored on periodical basis say weekly to save HO interest. Entries of draft cancellation should also be followed and reimbursement from related branches be claimed and received in time to save HO interest.

(16) *Government Business*

BM to ensure that fee/commission for handling Government business viz. pensions, direct and indirect taxes etc. have been received to boost profit.

(17) *Draft Issue Business*

Issue of draft business should be encouraged to increase income in the form of commission on draft.

(18) *Non-fund Business*

Non-fund business i.e. Rupee Traveller's cheques, gift cheques should be encouraged to attract more customers of good standing resulting increase in business and profit. In order to get more profit Inland bills business should also be captured by motivating traders of clothes, kirana, medicines, fertilizers etc. from places where the Bank has the branch-offices.

(19) *Recovery of Write-off Accounts*

BM to make sincere and continuous efforts for effective recovery in write-off accounts by personal contacts from borrowers and their friends/relatives etc. through compromise proposals. It will increase profits of branch office substantially.

(20) *Compromise Proposals*

BM to take sincere efforts for compromise in NPA accounts in order to boost recovery in these accounts as well as reduction in the volume of amount. It will also increase profit of the branch office.

In the end, I would like to say that profit is a basic need for any business unit/ concern for its existence and survival. Therefore, sincere and continuous efforts are essential for increase in profit of an enterprise.

23

Securities and Exchange Board of India

Genesis

India has had a long history of stock exchange with the Bombay Stock Exchange having been set-up as early as 1887. But the securities market really emerged from the periphery into the main stream of the country's financial system only since the beginning of last two decade. Thanks to the liberalisation process set into motion by the Govternment, resources raised from the market increased from around Rs. 160 crores in 1980-81 to over Rs. 4100 crores in 1986-87.

Fair and efficient securities market has an important role to play in country's industrialisation efforts. They directly affect mobilisation and efficient channeling of savings into productive enterprises. By offering attractive rewards, they encourage thrift and risk taking which help borrowing enterprises to raise money in cost-effective manner.

There has been a significant increase in awareness of, and interest in equity instruments among savers in recent years. This awareness and interest have, however, not yet crystallised into a committed, discerning and growing pool of providers of risk capital.

The main reasons for this are high volatility of market prices and the erosion of investor confidence which have become all the more apparent after the steep fall in prices in 1986. Several undesirable practices and structural inadequacies have contributed. To realize the full potential of the securities markets, and to channelise an increasing flow of funds into industry, investor confidence is to be restored and sustained. The inter-mediation would have to meet high standards of honesty, competence and solvency.

Presenting the Budget for 1986-87, the then Prime Minister declared:

"... .For a healthy growth of capital markets, investor's rights must be fully protected. Trading malpractices must be prevented. Government have decided to set up a separate Board for the regulation and orderly functioning of stock exchanges and the securities industry."

Accordingly, the Govt. constituted the Securities and Exchange Board of India (SEBI) on April 12,1988 to promote orderly and healthy development of the securities markets and to provide adequate investor protection.

Objectives

The Securities and Exchange Board of India would seek to create an environment to facilitate mobilisation of adequate resources through the securities markets. This environment includes rules and regulations, institutions and their inter-relationship, instruments, practices, infrastructure, policy framework and should have an overall sense of fairness. The markets must inspire confidence.

These objectives can be accomplished by being responsive to the needs of the three groups which basically constitute the market: (1) the issuers of securities. (2) the investors (3) the market intermediaries.

- To the issuers, it should afford a market place in which they can confidently look forward to raising all finance they need in an easy and efficient manner.

- To the investors, it would provide a high degree of protection of their rights and interests through adequate, accurate and authentic information and disclosure of information on a continuous basis. The market should be attractive, efficient, but above all fair.
- To the intermediaries, it should offer a competitive, professionalised and expanding market with adequate and efficient infrastructure so that they are able to render better service to the investors and the issuers.

Approach

In accomplishing its broad objectives, the Board needs to play a dual role in the securities markets by adopting regulatory functions as well as playing an important developmental role.

Regulatory and developmental functions are strongly interlinked and have the same objectives in the long run. Rapid and healthy development is very often an outcome of well-regulated structures. Regulation should be viewed as analogous to the rules needed to play a fair and exciting game of cricket, traffic rules for the safe and yet smooth flow of traffic, and orderly planting of seedlings to ensure that each one grows into a healthy plant. The regulatory measures subservient to the needs of development and just enough to enforce the required degree of discipline and fairness.

The Board would aim at creating effective surveillance mechanism for the securities markets, and encouraging responsible and accountable autonomy on the part of all players in the market. They should discipline themselves and observe the rules of the game.

Comprehensive Legislation

While the securities markets in the country have long been regulated, the approach has been segmented one with the existing regulation affecting securities markets spread over several acts: the Companies Act, Capital Issue (Control) Act, Securities Contracts (Regulation) Act and various rules, orders and notifications made thereunder. The system has become less than adequate in view of the substantial growth in the capital market activities, in investor population and growing complexities of market-regulated problems.

The first task of the Board is to evolve a comprehensive legislation covering all aspects of the securities markets in an integrated framework. It would consolidate and rationalise existing regulation and extend regulatory purview to areas where it is needed but does not exist. The purpose is to unify, rather than add up, and make it comprehensive and effective, rather than amend and enlarge. The new framework will aim it better investor safeguard through improved disclosure requirements, accounting standards, compensation and arbitration, small investor's protection fund, steps against insider trading and other malpractices.

Interim Functions

The Boards to begin with, has been formed as a non-statutory body to serve as a precursor to the proposed Statutory Board. It will be converted into a Statutory Board on passing of the Bill. It shall : (i) deal with all matters relating to the development and regulation of the securities markets and investors protection and advise Govt. on these matters. (ii) Prepare comprehensive legislation for the regulation and development of securities markets. (iii) Carry out such functions as may be delegated by the Central Govt. for the development and regulation of securities market in India.

Address of the Board

Securities and Exchange Board of India,
Nariman Bhavan, 14th Floor, Nariman Point,
Mumbai-400021.

24

Depository Services

Over the last 2 decades, the Indian Capital market has been growing by leaps and bounds. India has the largest number of listed companies in the world today. It also has a very large number of shareholders. With increase in volumes the problems associated with the settlements of trades are also on the rise. The large numbers in the capital market have also given rise to a large amount of paper work, bringing with it the associate problems.

The present system of settlement based on physical delivery of paper certificates was probably adequate in the past when only a handful of investors were participating in the capital market. But with swelling volume of transactions in the Bourses/ Stock Exchanges, the investors are facing delays in the settlement besides problems such as bad delivery, delay in registering transactions of transfer, loss/ misplacement of certificates in transit etc. The system of settlement based on physical deliveries has simply not been able to keep pace with the increased volumes.

In the scenario, it was felt that setting up a depository and introduction of scripless settlement would improve the efficiency of market thus, eliminating the various problems brought about by dealing in physical certificates. The Govt. of India enacted the Depositories Act in August 1996 paving the way for setting up of depository in India. National

Securities Depository Ltd (NSDL) was setup in 1996 to start the system of depositories. NSDL was promoted by UTI, IDBI and NSE.

For holding securities in the depository the two routes that are adopted the world over are:

(A) *Immobilisation* in which the securities are held by depositories in the physical form in its own vaults, but transfer of securities take place through book entries.

(B) *Dematerialisation (De-mat)* in which securities in physical form are shredded and corresponding credit is made in the form of electronic balance maintained with the depository. Account transfers are through book entries.

The law in our country has adopted the De-mat route. The De-mat securities are fungible, which means that all the holdings of a particular security are identical and interchangeable. The depository will, facilitate De-mat of securities. The investors have the option of holding securities in physical form or in the depository form.

He can also withdraw the securities from the depository by requesting issue of physical certificates.

The depository system is very similar to a banking environment. Thus, while a bank performs the functions of holding, transferring and allowing withdrawal of funds, a depository performs the functions of holding, transferring and allowing withdrawal of securities. Like a bank, a depository also reaches out to the general investor through its agents, which are called Depository Participants (DPs). Banks, financial institutions, registered stockbrokers and certain other categories can become DPs.

The depository system offers the following services:

(1) Maintain beneficial holdings

The depository, through DPs will maintain account

balances for investors that will reflect their portfolio of securities. The statement of holding is the statement of ownership of securities held in electronic form.

(2) Dematerialisation

In the depository system the physical certificates after verification by Registrars are destroyed and the number of shares is credited in the account. This is called dematerialization. Only shares registered in the name of account holders and of the companies who have entered into agreement with the depository i.e. NSDL are eligible for De-mat.

(3) Rematerialisation

This is conversion of electronic holdings back into physical form and issue fresh certificates. The investors has the option to withdraw from the Depository.

(4) Transfer

Receipts and delivery of securities in and from an investors account on purchase and sale of securities other than on Stock Exchange are done in the same way as credit and debit in a normal saving or current account with the bank.

(5) Trading and Settlement

For settlement of trades entered into through brokers and stock exchanges the depository inter-acts with the clearing corporation for delivery and receipt of obligation. Under the depository framework of settlement, NSDL does not move the securities from the delivery members to the receiving members until the clearing corporation confirms that the funds have been received. The depository system follows Rolling Settlement System (T+5), which means that if the broker executed the transaction on Monday, settlement of the same will take place on next Monday.

(6) Receipt of Corporation Benefits

NSDL provides details of the beneficial owners as on the record date to the company, to enable company, to calculate corporation benefits such as dividend, interest, bonus rights etc. arising out of beneficial holdings.

(7) Pledging/Hypothecation

NSDL provides the facility to pledge/ hypothecation the securities in De-met form in favour of lenders to enable the beneficial owners to borrow. The securities are then blocked in favour of the lenders.

Benefits

The depository system of holding and trading securities in electronic form offers the following benefits to investors and brokers:

(1) No risk of bad delivery:
(2) No delay in transfer of securities. The securities are transferred immediately in the name of purchaser.
(3) No execution of transfer-deed.
(4) No stamp duty on transfer of shares.
(5) Reduces handling of huge volumes of paper.
(6) Eliminates all risks associated with physical certificates such as loss, theft, mutilation, forgery etc.
(7) Reduces transaction cost.

To Brokers

(1) No more handling of cumbersome paper work thereby increasing scope for generating large volume of business.
(2) No risk for bad delivery.
(3) Savings in back office, man power etc.
(4) Can provide better services to its clients etc.

25

Mutual Funds

In this context,we feel that besides investment banks, institutions best suited to Indian Financial environment at present are mutual funds. "A mutual fund is a professionally managed company that combines the money of many people whose goals are similar." It invests funds collected in stocks and bonds to achieve the goals set for itself. "A mutual fund pools the savings of the community and invest them, after careful research and analysis, in various types of securities; offers the individual saver advantages of reasonable dividends and capital appreciation coupled with safety and liquidity."

Mutual funds are ideally suited the Indian financial environment. First, there is a preponderance of small investors in India, who have the ability to save. In recent years he is also willing to invest in shares and debentures, but hesitates to do so because of his lack of market information, his inability to reach the market quickly, difficulties he faces in transacting business and obtaining liquidity in the secondary market. In India even regular investors both individuals and institutions, do not possess requisite expertise needed for security analysis and for selecting appropriate investment portfolios. A need for professionally managed mutual funds has grown in recent years as stock exchanges are becoming more volatile and complex.

Second, the size of the investing population on Indian Stock Exchanges is quite large, it is the third largest next only to U.S. and Japan. What is more, it is expected to grow very fast as Indian Stock Exchanges reach maturity in a few years from the present nascent state. It is extremely difficult to arrange for direct individual participation on stock exchanges for investing population of this dimension. Indirect participation through mutual funds is an ideal solution to this problem.

Further, at present more than 90 per cent of the total value of shares and debentures is held by urban population residing in industrially advanced, educationally forward and financially sophisticated western region of the country. The population of the rest of the urban and the entire rural and semi-urban regions has command over an enormous pool of savings. Yet it is financially unsophisticated to deal directly with the stock exchanges. The stock exchanges in their turn do not have well developed administrative machinery to reach them. Under these circumstances mutual funds could be ideal financial intermediaries bringing investing population which is denied access to stock exchange due to various reasons and stock exchanges which are unable to reach them because of administrative inadequacies. In this context it must be noted that the recent launching of mutual funds by subsidiaries of some of the leading commercial banks which have a wide network of branches in rural and semi-urban areas is a step in right direction.

Third, in view of the deteriorating balance of trade situation and mounting debt-servicing burden, both of which are expected to continue in forceable future, it has increasingly become necessary to tap the savings of foreign investors (including non-resident Indians) directly. It is preferable to tap the foreign savings through a number of mutual funds since foreign investors have no expert knowledge about Indian Companies and rules and regulations (including FERA regulations) governing investments in India for efficient management of their portfolios. The Unit Trust of India has already floated India Fund and India Growth Fund to attract foreign funds from NRIs for investment in India. Another fund - Indian Investment Fund is promoted by Grindlay's Investment Services (Overseas) Ltd. The SBI capital market have also launched India Magnum Fund to cater to institutional investors in U.S.A.

Fourth, the various segments of the capital market, primary issue market, secondary markets in shares and debentures, markets for Giltedged Govt. Securities, even money markets could be developed and integrated into one financial market through operation of mutual funds which are active simultaneously on more than one market.

Fifth, a fund can be tailored to suit every purpose to cover the entire spectrum of investment requirements of the investors both domestic and foreign. In fact the scope for mutual funds is unlimited. In the U.S. the origional home of mutual funds 80 per cent of investments in securities is institutionalised, mostly in mutual funds. In the U.S. there were 1531 mutual funds with 30 million fund investors and $252 billion in assets at the end of 1985. The diversity of mutual funds in the U.S. can be gauged by the list of different funds given below in the descending order of risk:

(1) Aggressive Growth Funds.

(2) Growth Funds.

(3) Growth and Income Funds.

(4) Precious Metal Funds.

(5) International Funds.

(6) Balance Funds.

(7) Income Funds.

(8) Option/Income Funds.

(9) Government Bond Funds.

(10) Government National Mortgage Association Obligations Funds.

(11) Corporate Bond Funds.

(12) Municipal Bond Funds, and

(13) State Municipal Bond Funds.

India too, like the U.S. is a country of continental size with larger population and greater diversity of investing population. Thus there is a tremedous need and scope for a large variety of mutual funds in India. The Banking Regulation Act was amended in 1987 enabling commercial banks to set up subsidiaries which could be members of country's stock exchanges and operate as brokers and jobbers. The setting up of mutual funds by bank subsidiaries is a legal activity now. Government has extended the mutual funds similar tax advantages as those enjoyed by UTI. The list of investments in which mutual funds can legally operate is really very wide. It includes all types of shares, debentures, bonds of any company or corporate body. Company deposits, deposits with other corporate bodies, scheduled banks and similar institutions, commercial paper, Government securities belonging to Central, State and Local Governments, securities floated by foreign Government or foreign bank or any other authority outside India and approved by the RBI. SBI, Canara Bank, Indian Bank, PNB, Bank of India have successfully floated mutual funds. Among non-bank financial institutions like LIC, ICICI and GIC have entered the field of mutual funds. These recent developments augur well for future financial developments on capital markets in India. These various mutual funds including UTI have mobilised substantial resources from the market. Till Dec. 1989, the bank funds had a outstanding of Rs. 920.12 crores and UTI had over Rs. 11000 crores of investible funds.

Funds Abroad

The UTI was also the first to tap international investors. In 1986, it launched the India Fund, which is quoted at the London Stock Exchange. In 1988 July, it started the India Growth Fund quoted on the New York Stock Exchange. The initial subscription to the two funds was limited to Pound Sterling 128 million and also $ 60 million. The State Bank of India Capital Markets also launched its maiden offshore fund, India Magnum Fund NV, constituted in Netherlands Antilles. The fund targeted at institutional investors' in USA, mopped up $ 157 million against a target of $ 100 million.

However, in response to recent years world developments the scope of more Indian funds abroad is not too bright. The prospect of a single European Market has changed the priorities of European Merchant Bankers who are no longer interested in business outside the EEC, at least for the time being. A recent EEC directive called UCITS i.e. Undertakings for Collective Investments and Transferable Securities, allows reciprocity within the community as consequence of which European Institutions are concentrating on expanding their activities across European National boarders. Possibly America and Japan will prove to be better avenues for Indian funds abroad.

Regulatory Framework

Since mutual funds barring UTI are recent developments in the Indian financial scene there is lack of uniform regulation to cover various mutual funds. Banks' mutual funds are governed by RBI guidelines. UTI is subject to UTI Act 1964 and LIC has its own regulations for its mutual funds. Considering amount of resources that mutual funds have already mobilised and their inherent potential the need for a single regulatory authority is obvious. The existing anomalies in tax concessions available to different mutual funds could also be removed by such an authority.

The RBI guidelines applicable to banks cover the constitution and management, investment objectives and policies, prudential explosure: ceiling limits, pricing policy and income distribution, statement of accounts and disclosures.

The Future

The first acceptance of mutual funds in our financial market reveals the existing lacunae for such a profitable and relatively safe instrument. Their potential can be seen from the fact that resources raised in capital market form just 7 per cent of household savings and individual investors still do not form large percentage of mutual funds resources. However, the experiences of other countries show that with the development of capital markets more household savings are routed to secondary market through institutions like mutual funds. This trend is visible in case of UTI too. The share of household savings in UTI increased from 2.3 per cent in 1981 to 4.7 per cent in 1988. In Japan, 80 per cent of such savings are routed through institutions. Thus, once mutual funds gain credibility and faith among the common man, they are going to be a very significant force in the financial sector.

26

Stock Invest for Investors

In any forum seeking investor's woes the maximum number of complaints relate to non-repayment or inordinately delayed repayment of refunds. The Government is said to have received 30,000 complaints regarding non-payments of refund money on time from the investing public in the last few years. According to SEBI, one - third of the complaints it receives are on this account. It is estimated that at any point of time a sum of nearly Rs. 100 crores pending repayment is slashed off by companies, adversely affecting the liquidity position of lakhs of investors. This is in spite of stipulations under the Companies Act and CCI guidelines, laying down a timeframe for completion of allotment procedure, dispatch of allotment letters and refund orders. In such a situation something concrete to improve the situation was long overdue. Thus the new stock market instrument viz. Stock-Invest is certainly a very welcome one.

Stock-Invest mooted at the initiative of SEBI by State Bank of India is envisaged be an instrument just like a draft or a banker's cheque. Under the Stock Invest scheme an investor's account gets debited only upon the finalisation of the basis of allotment and in case of unsuccessful applicants, the accounts are not debited at all. The investor is, thus, obliged to part with his money only in case of successful total or partial allotment. Till, such allotment, the investor's funds remain in his account on which he will continue to earn interest. At present, stock invest is an additional facility for applying for primary issues and other existing instruments viz. cash, cheques and drafts continue to be operative. Stock invest is basically to be a non-negotiable instrument combining the features of a letter of authority and a guaranteed cheques. The currency of the instrument is six months.

Stock invest is issued in five denominations with ceiling for drawing up to Rs. 50, Rs. 500, Rs. 2500, Rs. 5000, Rs. 10000. The stock-invest form at the top specifies these various amounts. Bankers charge their commission on issue of stock-invest as per SEBI guidelines. Investors' money remains in their accounts, and earn interest, until the basis of allotment is decided. Only in case of successful allotment their accounts get debited. The excess application money in case of partial allotment also remains in the account.

The companies issuing shares is benefited greatly. For them, the eligible funds, once the basis of allotment is decided, will be credited to their account even before formal allotment is made. Further once this instrument takes off many more investors, who at present are hesitant to block their funds, will be ready to put in their money into new issues. As far as the Registrars to the issue are concerned their work relating to refund orders will become redundant. However, they will now have to provide safe custody for stock-invest forms and send the same back to banks after sorting. Still this additional work will be for less taxing than the earlier refund system.

The role of bank's in launching stock invest is very crucial. The very success of stock-invest is based on harnessing the vast branch network of commercial banks. Banks will be issuing the stock-invest to their customers (saving fund, fixed deposits or current account holders) at their request. It is envisaged to be made payable at all branches of the issuing bank. Once the basis of allotment is decided, the Registrar to the issue will send stock-invests to the branch of the collecting bank of public issues. After the company's account has been credited, the Registrar to the issue will proceed with formal allotment. In cases of successful allotment the Registrar to the issue will intimate the successful applicants, through allotment advice as per present practice. For unsuccessful applicants the Registrar will give a list of such forms along with cancelled, stock-invests to the controlling bank branches, which in turn will advise issuing branches in order to lift the lien from the investor's deposits. The issuing bank is then to advice the unsuccessful applicants accordingly. Once the instrument picks up, the bank can look forward to augmenting their resources through such a service. Also, the load on the clearing system will be much reduced, as only stock-invests of successful applicants will be presented through clearing. There will be no refund order too, further reducing an unnecessary burden on the clearing system. To begin with, State Bank is to undertake a pilot study for stock-invest at Hyderabad, for which it awaits IBA clearance. Other banks, viz. Punjab National Bank, Bank of Baroda, ANZ Grindlay's Bank and ABN Bank have also shown interest in the scheme.

The SEBI press note specifies that banks are to levy a service charge for stock-invest by "providing this facility as they do in case of drafts or TTs or mail orders." This implies that the cost of stock-invest will be in tandem with that for drafts, as it is the cost of a draft is highly subsidised by banks. The comparative cost for a draft and money order for a sum of Rs. 500 is Rs. 2 and Rs. 25 respectively. There seems to be no rationale for providing stock-invests at similar rates as those for drafts. It is essential that banks should have the freedom to charge a cost plus price for stock-invests to ensure that it is not an unwanted burden on them. The cost of stationery, personnel and responsibility involved need to be worked out for working out such a price. There is no danger of banks overcharging, due to competition amongst banks; in the present situation where deposits are hard to come by such competition is ensured.

The envisaged benefits of stock-invest rest largely on popularisation of stock-invests so as to replace other alternatives in the form of cash, cheques and drafts. Such a shift is again dependent on the cooperation and enthusiasm of the concerned agencies viz. banks, Registrar to the issue, as also on the vigilance of the authorities. The scheme as envisaged is no doubt good. However, it needs to be ensured that in case of deliberate misuse by any party concerned, severe retribution should be meeted out immediately. This will act as a deterrent to any willful malpractice. Such reprival falls within the realm of prudential controls and will come within the purview of SBI. Now the SEBI has been granted statutory recognition, it will hopefully be in a better position to effect such regulation.

Terms of Issue and Payment of Stock-Invest

(1) It is issued to the applicant, to be used for applying for new issues of shares/debentures/bonds only.

(2) The applicant will authorise payment of the maximum sum payable towards application money for shares/ debentures/bonds applied on the left hand side of stock-invest. The payee will fill in the actual amount receivable on the right hand side indicating the number of shares/debentures/bonds for which payment is appropriated. The amount shown on the right hand side will be equal to or less than the amount indicated on the left and should be within the overall ceiling of stock-invest, indicated on the right hand side.

(3) Stock-invest is paid on the payee filling in the required particulars on the right hand side under

due authorisation and discharge by their authorised signatory and presenting it for payment.

(4) Stock-invest is neither transferable nor negotiable. The issuing bank undertakes to pay the lower of the two sum indicated on the face of the instrument (representing the application money payable on his entitlement of shares/debentures/bonds according to the basis of allotment and his application) in terms of the authorisation given by the account holder herein. Payment will be made only by credit to the payee's account with their bankers.

(5) Stock-invest is current for six months from the date of its issue indicated on its face and no amount can be claimed on the stock-invest by the issuing bank branch unless it is presented to it within this six months.

(6) Stock-invest is payable at all branches of the issuing bank.

(7) Stock-invest is valid for payment only when signed by the issuing banker at the appointed place on its face.

(8) The account holder instructions to the bank, given herein, are irrevocable.

(9) It is understood that at the explicit undertaking of the account holder an amount equivalent to the sum mentioned on the left hand side of the stock-invest is either debited to his account or lien marked on his deposit account, from the date of its issue, till full liability under the stock-invest is extinguished.

(10) The bank shall not be liable for any delay, error, fraud, forgery or any other lapse in the issue or encashment of the stock-invest. It shall also be not liable for any losses/ damages in case of death, insanity or insolvency of the drawer before actual allotment/ delivery of the relative shares/ debentures/bonds by the payee company.

27

Non-resident Account

(I) Introduction and Objects

(a) Our Exchange Control covers all types of transactions (Physical and Invisible), persons and Accounts. One of the object of E.C Regulations is to check compensatory payments, smuggling and flight of capital from India. With this end in view, RBI controls the accounts of non-residents kept with banks in India. Sections 8 and 9 of FERA 1973 which form the legal basis for NR A/cs stipulate that payment and receipt of funds for and behalf of non-residents by any person in India cannot be done without the general or special permission of RBI.

(b) Under existing exchange control regulations there is NO BAR to receive inward remittance from abroad either through normal banking channels or in person. Travellers bringing foreign exchange more than equivalant of US $1000 have to declare to Customs on Currency Declaration Form (CDF). In case an inward remittance exceeds Rs. 10,000/ AD (Authorised Dealer) has to send a supplementary statement to RBI giving inter-alia, "Purpose of Remittance."

(II) Definition

1. Resident

Sec (2) (P) of FERA 1975 defines resident, a person who is:

(i) a citizen of India staying in India AFTER 25.3.1947 (i.e. when first FERA 1947 became effective).

(ii) FOREIGN NATIONAL (i.e. foreign passport holder) who is staying in India for employment or vocation/ occupation/business.

(iii) FOREIGN CITIZEN who is in India as DEPENDENT on (b) i.e. "Spouse".

(iv) Any person who is staying in India for any OTHER PURPOSE, which clearly indicates his intention to stay in India for an INDEFINITE PERIOD.

Note: (a) Offices and branches of foreign companies, firms, banks or any other organisations functioning in India and (b) Bhutanees and Nepalese residing in India, Nepal and Bhutan are treated as Residents.

2. Non-Residents

Section 2(q) of FERA 1973 defines Non-Resident, as a person who is not a resident in India and the following persons are treated as non-residents

(i) Indian citizens who stay abroad for employment, business/vocations and their dependents including Government Servants posted abroad for various assignments in India Embassies/UNO/ World Bank, etc.

(ii) Emmigrants.

(iii) Branches of Indian Companies/Firms/Banks functioning outside India.

(iv) Indian citizens residing abroad INDEFINITE PERIOD of stay for any other purpose.

Note:

(a) If AD* has doubt regarding the determination of residential status of a person, he should refer to RBI the case with full available particulars.

(b) Indian citizens who proceed abroad for higher studies, short-business visits, training etc. continue to be treated as persons RESIDENT IN INDIA.

(c) Indian origin foreign nationals are those persons who were born in India or have an Indian heritage through their parents, fore-fathers and are holding passports issued by foreign countries.

(d) Income Tax Act-1961, Indian Companies Act or any other Act will NOT affect the definition of a Resident/ Non-Resident provided by FERA-1973.

ADs Responsibility for N/R Accounts

ADs responsibility is to ensure that when a person becomes a Non-Resident, his account should be designated as NR A/c and when he becomes a resident, his account should be redesignited as Resident account. It is the duty of the account holder to inform his banker when his residential status changes. Sometimes, RBI and enforcement directorate also advise the banks to convert a Resident A/c into NR A/c. At times banks themselves come to know that the account holder has become a non-resident.

(III) Types of Non-Resident Accounts

(1) Non-Resident Bank Accounts.
- (i) Convertible (Rs)
- (ii) Inconvertible (Rs)

(2) Non-Resident Private accounts
- (i) Ordinary (Rs)
- (ii) External (Rs)

---

* AD = Authorised Dealer in foreign currency.

(iii) Foreign Currency

(iv) Blocked (Rs)

(1) NON-RESIDENT BANK ACCOUNTS of overseas branches can be opened with ADs in India WITHOUT prior approval of RBI. These accounts are used for settling trade transactions and remittances in an economical and convenient way. CONVERTIBLE BANK. Accounts are in respect of countries failing under "A Group" i.e. external account countries and INCONVERTIBLE ACCOUNTS belong to Bilateral account countries like USSR with whom India has Rupee trade. Both Account is freely transferable while from Inconvertible Account, transfers are limited between the two countries. Any credit/debit to these accounts tantamounts to a remittance/ receipt of foreign exchange and AD should ensure that only those transactions are put through these accounts which are otherwise permissible by the control.

(2) Non-Resident Private Accounts

(i) ORDINARY ACCOUNT is kept with ADs in rupees for Indians, foreigners and companies/firms who are treated as non-residents. It can be opened either by a REMITTANCE in foreign exchange or transfer of existing accounts. Funds in this accounts CANNOT be repatriated abroad without the prior permission of RBI - IN NO CASE credits are allowed. Income-tax (currently) 36 per cent should be deducted on interest earned/accrued AT SOURCE by the AD for credit to Govt. of India accounts, Operations i.e. withdrawals for LOCAL expenses are freely allowed if balance in any of the accounts (i.e. FDR, SB accounts) does not exceed Rs. 50,000.

RBI has empowered the ADs to allow certain operations on this accounts WITHOUT permission of

RBI (details of which are in ECM). This account can be used for payment of passage fare (for the non-resident and his dependents) to INDIAN carriers with RBI's permission. Investments in immovable property and in companies / firms etc. are also permissible on NON-REPATRIATION basis. Recently, RBI has permitted the ADs to credit rents received from the residents to the NR A/cs WITHOUT PRIOR permission of RBI. Insurance premia and Govt. dues can be made without limit. Power of Attorney can also be given to the residents for operation of Non-Resident Accounts, Joint Non-resident Accounts with the RESIDENTS are also permissible with/ without RBI's permission.

(ii) NON-RESIDENT EXTERNAL ACCOUNT : (NRE A/cs) Non-Resident External account can be opened by ADs only in the names of INDIAN NATIONALS or persons of INDIAN ORIGIN resident OUTSIDE India provided funds for the purpose represent INWARD REMITTANCE in foreign exchange received in an approved manner. No local credits in Indian Rupees are permissible. This account has a number of advantage viz:

(a) Tax exemption - both Income-tax and wealth tax free.

(b) No restriction on local withdrawals and opening of FDR A/cs.

(c) Repatriation of balances with interest allowed without RBI's approval.

(d) Priority sector items i.e. scooter, etc. can be purchased by debit to this account.

(e) Investments in Units of UTI and Govt. securities allowed with repatriation benefits.

(f) Other investments are allowed only with RBI's permission.

(iii) FOREIGN CURRENCY NON-RESIDENT ACCOUNT (FCNR)

To cover the risk of any loss arising from FLUCTUATIONS IN EXCHANGE rate of currencies vis-a-vis the Indian Rupees, RBI has with effect from 01-11-1975 allowed opening of FCNR Accounts in the name of INDIANS in TWO foreign currencies vis. £(UK) and $(USA). ADs can open these accounts WITHOUT RBI's approval and all the advantages of NRE account are available, IN ADDITION a cover for rate fluctuations. Foreign exchange received for credit to these account is sold to RBI by ADs, at a notional rate and RBI will resell the exchange at the same rate (the loss being borne by RBI).

This account is permissible to be kept in TERM Deposits only.

(iv) BLOCKED ACCOUNTS

Non-resident blocked account can be opened and operated by ADs. ONLY with the PRIOR PERMISSION of RBI. Payments due to non-residents belonging to enemy countries like Rhodesia etc. and irregular foreign exchange transaction are directed by RBI to be credited to the blocked account. A credit to a Blocked a/c is treated as a valid discharge for the debt.

Note: All the above four types of accounts can be opened by ADs simultaneously in the name of same non-resident.

(v) OTHER ACCOUNTS

(a) Form QA-22 is required to be completed by a foreign national if he opens an account with AD. The object of this form is to bring to the notice of FOREIGN national company that it is an offence to make foreign exchange available to residents of India against reimbursement in rupees.

(b) FOREIGN TOURIST ACCOUNTS : ADs can open NON RESIDENT ACCOUNTS for foreign tourists for SIX months provided the funds in the A/c represent only the proceeds of foreign exchange and QA - 22 form is completed.

(c) FOREIGN STUDENTS: Foreign students can open RESIDENT account with ADs on completion of QA 22 form provided the accounts funded with inward remittances from abroad or by stipend/ scholarship paid by Govt. of India. When student leaves India on completion of studies, ADs can themselves allow a remittance upto $ 500 out of this a/c and for the balance refer to RBI.

(d) DIPLOMATIC BOND STORE ACCOUNT (DBS A/c) Foreign Embassies/diplomats in India can open DBS A/cs with ADs WITH THE PERMISSION OF RBI for the purchase of duty-free goods from Bonded Stores. This account is funded with proceeds of inward remittances from abroad and NO LOCAL CREDITS are permitted.

(e) FOREIGN DIPLOMATES/UNO AND OTHER INTERNATIONAL INSTITUTIONS ACCOUNTS Foreign Diplomates/UNO and other International Institutions accounts can be opened WITHOUT prior approval of RBI and without completion of QA 22 Forms. These a/cs are treated as RESIDENT accounts.

(f) NON-CONVERTIBLE account is opened by ADs in favour of Res idents/Non-residents to facilitate purchase of priority sector items, like scooter etc. The funds in this a/c represent proceeds of inward remittances ONLY and balances in this a/c cannot be transferred abroad.

28

Small Industries Development Bank of India (SIDBI)

Small Industries Development Bank of India (SIDBI) was set up on April 2, 1990 under the Act of Parliament. Its functions include promotion, financing and development of the Micro, Small and Medium Enterprise (MSME) Sector and coordinate the functions of the institutions engaged in similar activities.

The authorised capital of SIDBI is Rs. 1000 crore. The paid up capital is Rs. 450 crore which is held by 35 financial institutions/public sector banks/insurance companies owned or controlled by Government of India. SIDBI completed 27 years service to the MSME sector on April 2, 2013. The cumulative disbursements of SIDBI since inception, up-to March 31, 2009 stood at Rs. 132412 crore.

Activities of SIDBI

SIDBI started as refinancing institution, emerged as complete financial institution meeting all needs of MSME sector for financial and support services.

Indirect Finance

The indirect financial assistance is extended in the form of refinance support to more than 900 Primary Leading

Institutions (PLIs), comprising banks, Small Financing Corporations (SFCs), Small Industries Development Corporations (SIDCs) etc. having a network of over 82000 branches and Microfinance support to over 140 microfinance institutions (MFIs) all over the country. Apart from PLIs, SIDBI also provides resource support to non-banking finance companies (NBFCs) to reach out to MSMEs not covered by the formal banking system. SIDBI also provides financial assistance to MFIs for onward leading microfinance services to the poor especially women.

Direct Finance

SIDBI started its direct finance with the objective that no bankable project in MSME sector should languish for want of resources. Accordingly direct finance is provided to fill in the credit gaps by way of supplementing and complementing the efforts of the banks/SFCs/MFIs to meet adequate credit needs of MSMEs at affordable rates.

Over the years, SIDBI has evolved itself as a one-stop institution to meet the various types of credit requirements of the MSME sector by directly offering tailor-made fund based and non-fund based financial projects and services. Direct finance is done through its Present network of 103 branches all over India covering more than 600 MSME clusters.

29

Corporate Governance in PSBs

The earliest definition of Corporate Governance stated that "the purpose of Corporate Governance is to conduct business in accordance with owner or share-holder's desires, which generally will be to make as much money as possible, while conforming to the basic rules of society embodied in law and local customs"—Milton Friedman. This definition stresses the economic concept of market value maximisation and champions the cause of share-holder capitalism over a period of time the definition of Corporate Governance has been widened to encompass the interests of not only share-holders but also other stake holders, e.g., customers, employees, suppliers, dealers, government, society etc.

The modern definition of Corporate Governance as advocated by the OECD, defines Corporate Governance as the system by which business corporations are directed and controlled. According to them the Corporate Governance structure specifies the distribution of rights and responsibilities among different participants in the corporation, such as, the Board, managers, shareholders and other stake-holders and spells out the rules and procedures for making decisions on corporate affairs. By doing this it provides the structure through which the company objectives are set and also provides the means of attaining those objectives and monitoring performance. Essentially it is "about promoting corporate fairness, transparency and accountability".

—J. Wolfensolin, President, World Bank

Corporate Governance mainly consists of two elements, (i) a long term relationship, which has to deal with checks and balances, incentives of managers and communication between management and investors and (ii) transactional relationship involving matters relating to disclosures and authority. This implies that Corporate Governance deals with laws, procedures, practices and implicit rules that determine a company's stability to take managerial decision vis-à-vis its various constituents, particularly its share-holders, creditors, state and employees. Corporate Governance refers to an economic, legal and institutional effort that allows companies to diversify, grow, restructure and exit and to do everything necessary to maximize long-term share holder value.

Corporate Governance in Banking Sector

Banks are a critical component of any economy and provide finance to commercial enterprises as also basic financial services to the general public. They also facilitate the payments mechanism in the systems. Banks are expected to make credit and liquidity available in difficult market conditions.

From a banking industry perspective, corporate governance involves the manner in which the business and affairs of individual institutions are governed by their Board of Directors and Senior Management, affecting how banks set corporate objectives including generating economic returns to owners, run the day-to-day operation of the business that seek to protect the interests of recognised stake-holder; align corporate activities and behaviour with the expectation that banks will operate in safe and sound manner, and in compliance with applicable laws and regulations; and more importantly protect the interests of depositors. The quality of corporate governance is essentially determined by the manner in which top management, particularly Board of Directors, allocates the financial resources to the company as between themselves and other interest groups such as employees, customers, government etc. The basic qualities invariably expected in this regard are trust, honesty, integrity, transparency and compliance with the laws of the land. There is an increasing body of public opinion that deems a business enterprise not merely as an economic unit but also as a good corporate citizen.

The RBI has taken great initiative in bringing about desired changes in governance in banks. Various committees and papers were introduced viz. principles for the management of interest rate risk (September 1997), Frame work for internal control systems in banking organisations (September 1998), principles for the management of credit risk (July 1999), enhancing bank transparency (September 1998), Basel Committee, Risk Management Committee, Audit Committee, Compensation Committee nominations committee, Advisory Group on Banking supervision (Chairman, Prof. M.S. Verma) Cadbury Committee, Kumar Mangalam Committee etc. by the Government of India and RBI in this regard.

PART – IV

30

Emergence of ATM in Banking Sector

Introduction

The Automated Teller Machine (ATM) is seen everywhere. This machine has brought innovations in banking sector all over the world.

The customers are no more dependent on the brick and mortar branch of a Bank. The advent of the ATM has made the concept of "24 × 7–365 days banking" a reality. The ATM has been helpful to both the bankers and the customers. The long crowd of customers in the banking hall of a bank's branch waiting for their turn to collect cash is disappearing. The branch business timings have lost significance to the customer after the introduction of the ATM.

The ATM is a device used by bank customers to process account transactions. The customer inserts into the ATM, a plastic card that is encoded with information on a magnetic strip. The strip contains an identification code that is transmitted to the bank's central computer by modem. Every card holder would be given a PIN (personal identification number) that he should enter and after verifying the same with the records, the ATM would allow operations.

History of ATM

ATM is also known as "Automated Banking Machine", "Cash Machine", "Cash Dispenser", "Automatic Teller" or "Money Machine".

The origin of ATM can be traced back to June 1967 when Barclays Bank installed the first Cash Dispenser (CD) manufactured by Burroughs in the U.K. The race commenced when just forty-eight hours later. National Westminster Bank commissioned a machine manufactured by Chubb. Since then, there have been rapid developments both in ATM hardware and software.

Chemical Bank installed the first ATM in 1969 at its branch in Rockville Centre, N. Y. A. Customer using a coded card was dispensed a package containing a net sum of money.

In 1971, Don Wetzel brought a more advanced ATM that was similar to current days ATM. Apart from payment of cash it also performed the functions of accepting cash, transferred money to different accounts etc.

ATM's in India

Hongkong and Shanghai Banking Corporation installed the first ATM in India in 1987 at Kolkata. Indian Bank was the first public sector bank to install an ATM in India. These were all standalone ATMs.

In February 1997, the Indian Bank's Association promoted a network of ATMs in Mumbai called 'SWADHAN' providing facility of cash withdrawal at ATMs of any of the member banks. This was the first major attempt in India to provide networked ATM services. 'Swadhan' was implemented first in Mumbai. However, it had its limitations.

The advent of new generation private sector banks in India gave a flip to the creation of ATM networks as these banks relied work on ATMs as the delivery channel instead of branch banking which was the forte of the traditional Indian Banks–both in the public sector and the private sector.

In response to the aggressive use of technology by the new generation banks and to meet the expectations of customers, the traditional Indian Banks also resorted to the creation of technology driven delivery channels, including the ATM channel.

Important manufacturers of ATM in the world are Triton, NCR and Diebold.

Types of Plastic Money

(i) *ATM Card*: This card would be useful only to operate the ATM.

(ii) *Debit Card:* This card would be useful to make payments for purchases for Member Establishments (MEs) who have arrangements with the card issuing agency/bank. All card issuers are affiliated to two major issuers VISA and Master Card.

(iii) *Debit cum ATM Card*: This is most common nowadays. The same card can be used to draw cash from ATM and also make payments to shops for purchases. This is a Two-in-One card.

(iv) *Credit Card*: This card enables the client (customer) to obtain goods or services from various shops have arrangements with the issuing agency/bank even when there is no balance in his savings or current account. Normally a limit would be fixed—based on net worth of the client—upto which the client can use the card. The same card can be used even to draw cash from ATMs within the cash limit approved to that client. Normally, at the time of issuing the card, they would intimate the client two limits (spending limits) – One the total spending limit (based on the net worth of the client and the other sublimit within the total spending limit for the purpose of drawing cash. For example, a card may have a total spending limit of Rs. 1 Lac with a sub-limit for cash withdrawal of Rs. 20000.

The functions performed by Debit and Credit Cards are same. The only difference is that the transactions can be put through if and only if balance is available in the customer's account (SB/CD) but in credit cards even without balance in the account, the client can operate-subject of course to the maximum limit fixed. (The bank/Agency would intimate this limit to the client at the time of issuing the card-this varies from client to client).

Credit Cards are normally valid in the country of issue. For example, the Credit Cards issued by banks in India, would be valid throughout India. If the Bank has arrangements with agencies in foreign countries, it may issue a credit card to select client which would be valid abroad as well. Such cards are termed "International Credit Cards."

Functions of ATM – The function of ATM differ from Bank to Bank. The following features are available in the ATM of all the Banks:

(i) *Fast Cash*: When you want to do the only activity of drawing cash in pre-determined amounts like Rs. 1000, 2000, 5000 etc. you can use this option.

(ii) *Normal Cash withdrawal*: Every bank has fixed a maximum limit of cash withdrawal per account per day. It ranges between Rs. 10-15000. While in some banks the maximum limit (amount) may be drawn in one shot (HDFC, ICICI), in other banks though Rs. 15000 is permitted per day, it should be drawn in lots of Rs. 5000 (Syndicate Bank) – that means we have to key in withdrawal of Rs. 5000 three times. All withdrawals should be in multiples of Rs. 100 only.

(iii) *Balance Enquiry*.

(iv) *Mini-Statement of Account*: You get details of 5-10 transactions.

(v) *PIN Change*.

(vi) *Cash Deposit*: Varied procedures exist. Here special covers are available in the ATM wherein the client has to fill up the challan, the denominations and key in these details. Then a window opens wherein the cover containing the cash has to be dropped. At the end of the day, officials of the bank's branch to which the ATM is attached, would open the machine, take the cover and credit the amount in the account of the customer. If there is any difference between the amount fed and actual cash in the cover, the decision of the bank is final.

(vii) *Return Card/ Cancel*.

(viii) *Transfer Transaction*: If you want to transfer funds with the Bank i.e., from one account to another account at the same branch or at different branch, you can use this option.

(ix) *Others* like request for Cheque Book, Statement of Account etc.

Advantages of ATM

To Banks are as under:

(1) Less space is required.

(2) Capital expenditure is lower compared to branch expenditure.

(3) Lower transaction cost.

(4) One more means for advertising Bank's products.

(5) Bank staff gets more time to do marketing.

To the Customers are as under:

(1) Convenience of Shopping. No need to carry cash.

(2) No need to visit branch for transactions.

(3) AAA Banking–Anytime, Anywhere, Anyhow

(4) Fast and efficient service.

(5) Good currency Notes (Fresh/Decent).

Future of ATM: Although ATM machines were originally developed as cash dispensers (CD), they have evolved to include many other bank-related functions. In future, ATMs may perform functions that are not directly related to the management of one's own bank account, such as paying routine bills, fees, legal fees, taxes, utilities, phone bills, social security etc. Loading monetary value into pre-paid cards (cell phones), Ticket purchases (train, concert), etc.

ATMs have a great role to play in India. All Banks have come together through an arrangement by which each bank's customer can access the ATMs of other Member Banks without any extra cost. This would ensure lower costs to the bank and higher and efficient utilisation of already installed ATMs. The National Financial Switch (NFS) network, which is owned and maintained by the Institute for Development and Research in Banking Technology, is the technical arm of the RBI and aims at linking all ATMs in the country for providing efficient and cheaper ATM operations. Many Public and Private Sector Banks are becoming members of NFS to get the benefits of over 9000 ATMs.

The cost of ATM has drastically come down over the past about 5 years. From an average original investment of Rs. 15 lacs, it has been reduced to Rs. 9 lacs. In addition, a recurring cost of Rs. 1 lac per month has to be incurred. With this cost pattern, around 180 transactions (technically called 'hits') per day are required to Break-even.

The cost of each transaction at the Branch of the Bank is Rs. 60 while it is Rs. 10 if carried out through ATM.

Efforts are on to manufacture ATMs that could be supplied around Rs. 2 lacs. This would help taking the ATM to the rural areas of the country. To suit the rural people and also as an additional security device innovations are being made in the form of using camera inside the ATM which could picture the client and compare with his records or use Thumb Impressions (Biometric) of the client for identification etc. Even, speaking ATMs are on trial and if introduced it would identify the client on recognizing his voice.

Thus, the ATM would be the 'Banking of the Future' and the brick and mortar branches would slowly disappear. Both the Bankers and the clients, due to its various benefits, have adapted themselves to the ATM culture.

31

An Era of Computerisation of Banks

The first initiative in the area of bank computerisation stemmed out of the landmark report of the two committees headed by Dr. R.C. Rangarajan the then governor of the RBI in 1980. Dr. R.C. Rangarajan strongly recommended computerisation of banking sector to increase transparency, accuracy, efficiency in work, better customer service and cost, time and man-power saving in banks. He recommended computerisation in banking operations at various levels and suggested appropriate architecture, as a measure to meet the winds of change.

Rangarajan Committee (I)

In early 1980, a high level committee was appointed under the chairmanship of Dr. C. Rangarajan, to draw up phased plan for computerisation and the mechanisation in the banking industry over a period of 5 years i.e. 1985-89. The focus was on customer service and two models of bank's branch automation were developed and implemented- front office in mechanisation where front desk operations were computerised while back office was done manually, and back office automation covering mechanisation of general ledger and back office operations like statements, day book etc. while the front office work was done manually.

Both the models provided the customer with error-free (complete accuracy) accounting, regular statement of accounts/pass-books etc. These were the major achievements in banking history of transformation but did not go far enough and the pace of their implementation was found tardy.

Also, some opposition from trade unions of banks existed considering the fear of unemployment or under-employment, retrenchment etc.

Rangarajan Committee (II)

The second Rangarajan committee formed in 1988 drew a detailed perspective plan for computerisation in banks and for extension of automation to other areas like funds transfer, electronic mail, BANK NET, SWIFT, ATM etc. The committee recommended the following path for computerisation over the period of next five years:

Around 2000 to 2500 large branches located at high activity (urban and metropolitan) centres to be fully computerised.

Computerization of regional offices/area offices/ divisional offices and head offices.

Inter and intro transactions using the BANK NET setup by the RBI and Installation of a network of cash dispensers (CDs)/ATMs at strategic locations such as airports/ railway stations, hospitals/ bus stands/ courts etc. on a shared basis by banks.

The committee had also recommended 'single window concept' 'all bank credit cards', credit clearing/GIRO System, office automation, etc. In fact this report was the most comprehensive road map for the automation considering the state of technology at that time.

32

Consolidation in Banks through Mergers and Acquisitions

Concepts of Mergers and Acquisitions

For a layman the words mergers, acquisitions, take over, amalgamation, consolidation etc. all may be similar but technically these are different. In fact, all these are various ways or methods by which the corporate restructuring can be done.

Clarification of Concepts

Merger: Merger is defined as combination of two or more companies into a single company where one survives and the other(s) lose(s) their/its corporate existence. The survivor acquires the assets as well as liabilities of the merged company or companies.

It can also be defined as the fusion of two or more existing companies. All assets, liabilities and stock of one company stand transferred to transferee company in consideration of payment in the form of equity shares of transferee Company or debentures or cash or a mix of these modes.

Acquisition: Acquisition is the purchase by one company of controlling interest in the share capital of another existing company. This means that even after the takeover although there is change in the management both the firms retain their separate legal identity.

Amalgamation: Amalgamation has been described by Halsburys law of England as a blending of two or more existing undertakings into one undertaking, the share holders of each blending company becoming substantially the share holders in the company which is to carry on the blending undertaking.

Takeover: A takeover is generally involves the acquisition of a certain block of equity capital of a company which enables the acquirer to exercise control over the affairs of the company.

Under the monopolies and restrictive trade practices act, takeover means acquisition of not less than 25 per cent of voting powers in a corporate.

Categories of Merger and Acquisition

Merger and acquisition depends upon propose, the offer company wants to achieve. Based on the offerer's objective profile, combinations could be horizontal, vertical or conglomeritic etc.

1. Horizontal Merger: Horizontal merger is a merger of two competing firms which are in the same line of business. The main purpose of such merger is to obtain economies of scale in production by eliminating duplication of facilities and operations and broadening the product line, elimination of competition, reduction of cost, increase in market segments and exercise of better control on market.

2. Vertical Merger: Vertical merger is a merger of one company with another which is involved in a different stage of production and/or distribution process thus espousing backward integration to assimilate the sources of supply and/or forward integration towards market outlets. The main motives are to ensure ready take off of the materials, gain control over product specifications, increase profitability by gaining the margins of the previous supplier/distributor, gain control over scare raw material supplies.

3. Conglomerate Merger: Conglomerate merger is an amalgamation of two companies engaged in different lines of business. The motive is to ensure better utilisation of financial resources, enlarge debt capacity, and to reduce risk by diversification.

Difference between Merger and Acquisition

Basically, there is no difference between merger and acquisition. Both relate to an investment in acquisition of a bank/company. The difference lies only in operational process of acquisition. In merger, one bank gets merged with the other losing its own identity by way of share transactions/ asset/liability transfers. In acquisition/takeover, one company/ a group of companies acquires the controlling interest on ownership of capital without making any corporation to lose its own individual identity. But in the eyes of law, the operation process marks a big difference. While merger is covered regulated /covered by the Companies Act, 1856, the acquisition/take over is regulated covered by the takeover norms prescribed by SEBI. As such, the process is supervised by the High Court and the Registrar of Companies, while the process of acquisition /takeover is undertaken as per norms of SEBI.

Difference between Acquisition and Takeover

Although we use the term acquisition and takeover interchangeably but in fact the term take over generally show a hostile act. To put in simple words, when an acquisition is forced or unwilling act, then it is called takeover.

Objective behind Mergers and Acquisitions

The probable objectives behind mergers and acquisitions in banking industry may be highlighted as under:

1. To overcome the problem of slow pace of growth and profitability due to widening of banking industry. The public sector banks have now to compete both with the private banks and the foreign banks both in terms of products and service parameters.
2. To revive a loss making bank as it may not be able to restore the non-performing assets (NPAs) are its own.
3. To utilise the underutilised market power in terms of regional and geographical coverage in the best possible manner.
4. To achieve some sort of diversification. (This happens when the merger is vertical or conglomerate).
5. To limit competition and prevent overcrowding and mushrooming up of many banks.
6. To gain economies of scale and increase income in proportion to less amount of investment.
7. To utilise underutilised resources. The resources include human, physical or managerial skills.
8. To carve the niche of oneself as a strategic empire builder and - amass vast economic power.

To end up, the word 'merger' may be taken as an abbreviation which means:

M = Mixing
E = Entities
R = Resources for
G = Growth
E = Enrichment and
R = Renovation

The factors favouring growth, enrichment and renovation should be taken into due consideration before stepping into the process of M & As. So that the abbreviation truly comes out to be fruitful.

Only the Indian banking industry will be able to stand right forth the global competition hurricane.

Merger and Acquisition in Banking Industry

The concept of corporate restructuring commonly known as Mergers and Acquisitions (M & As) in Asian countries, took its birth in America somewhere in 1890. Till date about two-third of very large public corporation in USA have had mergers in the corporate history. It remained confined to their territories till the mid seventies. As far as India is concerned, hats off to the liberalisation of FERA, MRTP and industrial licensing. The compulsions have become extremely competitive and the corporate (both business and service) are seriously thinking over M & As to compete both nationally and internationally. Earlier this concept was confined to only business corporations. But now, since there is a boom in the service sector, the concept has crept into the banking industry as well.

The banking system in India went through various stages before it emerged into modern banking system. With increase in trading and administration of East India Company, the early banking system of banias, chetty, sahukars, podars and shroffs was replaced by banks established by English agency houses during the end of eighteenth century. But almost all of them failed due to failure of parent agency houses during the trading crisis of 1829-33 as they mixed banks with trading.

The next setback by the banks was faced during 1862-65 during American civil war, which led to speculating boom in Indian cotton trade, as a result of which many banks and companies were formed. Although almost all of them failed as soon as the civil war was over and the boom collapsed. The three presidency banks set up by the respective governments, also failed due to handicap of inexperience and their inability to conduct foreign exchange business.

Under the impetus of Swadeshi Movement, the hitherto slow growth of Indian banking picked up pace, and between 1900-1914, a large number of new banks came up. Further the growth of Indian banking suffered its first and major setback in 1913, during the worst ever banking crisis in India, starting before the war and accentuated by it followed by post war depression (1922-23) wherein the rate of bank failure was very high and thereafter followed by incident of partition during 1947. Probably till that time no proper attention was paid to rescue these banks besides proper controlling and monitoring to check the failures.

After 1951, with the emergence of Reserve Bank of India as a decisive factor armed with new power it acquired in 1949 under Banking Companies Act to intervene in the event of crisis in a bank, the picture totally changed.

According to Section 45, the Reserve Bank of India can submit a scheme to the central government for amalgamation of a banking unit with a well managed bank within a period of not more than six months moratorium granted by the government on an application made earlier in that behalf by the Reserve Bank. The new Section 45 was inserted in Banking Companies Act in September 1960.

Thus, in 1961 alone thirty banks were merged compulsorily with other banks. As a consequence of improved atmosphere, bank failure decreased, while the number of mergers, amalgamation and transfers increased from one in 1954 to twenty-two in 1963 and seventy nine in 1964.

The idea behind this merger was to strengthen the banking system. Small, weak and inefficient non-scheduled banks which could hardly, if ever have become viable and eligible for a license, were being merged with other scheduled bank.

It is evident that the basic objective of banks merger or amalgamation was to check the frequent failure of banks and to save them from facing crisis and maintaining public confidence.

The list of banks merged since 1961 to 2004 is given below in Table 1 and Table 2:

Table: 1

Sr. No.	*Name of Bank Merged*	*With Whom Merged*	*Date of Merger*
1.	Prabhat Bank Ltd.	National Bank of Lahore Ltd.	09-03-1961
2.	Indo-Commercial Bank Ltd.	Punjab National Bank	25-03-1961
3.	Bank of Nagpur Ltd.	Bank of Maharashtra	27-03-1961
4.	New Citizen Bank Ltd.	Bank of Baroda	29-04-1961
5.	Travancore Forward Bank Ltd.	State Bank of Travancore	15-05-1961
6.	Bank of Kerala Ltd.	Canara Bank	20-05-1961
7.	Bank of Poona Ltd.	Sangli Bank Ltd.	03-06-1961
8.	Bank of New India Ltd.	State Bank of Travancore	17-06-1961
9.	Venadu Bank Ltd.	South Indian Bank Ltd.	17-06-1961
10.	Wankaner Bank Ltd.	Dena Bank	17-06-1961
11.	Seasia Midland Bank Ltd.	Canara Bank	17-06-1961
12.	Kottayam Orient Bank Ltd.	State Bank of Travancore	17-06-1961
13.	Bank of Konkan Ltd.	Bank of Maharashtra	19-06-1961
14.	Poona Investors Bank Ltd.	Sangli Bank	28-06-1961
15.	Bharat Industrial Bank Ltd.	Bank of Maharashtra	01-07-1961
16.	Rayalaseema Bank Ltd.	Indian Bank	01-09-1961
17.	Cuttack Bank Ltd.	United Bank of India	04-09-1961
18.	Pie Money Bank Pvt. Ltd.	Syndicate Bank	04-09-1961
19.	Moolky Bank Ltd.	Syndicate Bank	04-09-1961
20.	Merchants Bank Ltd.	Tanjore Permanent Bank Ltd.	04-09-1961
21.	Tezpur Industrial Bank Ltd.	United Bank of India	04-09-1961
22.	G. Raghunathmull Bank Ltd.	Canara Bank	04-09-1961
23.	Satara Swadeshi Commercial Bank Ltd.	United Western Bank Ltd.	06-09-1961
24.	Catholic Bank Ltd.	Syndicate Bank	11-09-1961
25.	Phaltan Bank	Sangli Bank Ltd.	07-10-1961
26.	Jodhpur Commercial Bank Ltd.	Central Bank of India	16-10-1961
27.	Bank of Citizen Ltd.	Canara Banking Corporation Ltd.	17-10-1961
28.	Karur Mercantile Bank Ltd.	Laxmi Vilas Bank Ltd.	19-10-1961
29.	Peoples Bank Ltd.	Syndicate Bank	14-11-1961
30.	Pratap Bank Ltd.	Lakshami Commercial Bank Ltd.	11-12-1961
31.	Unity Bank Ltd.	State Bank of India	20-08-1962
32.	Bank of Algapuri Ltd.	Indian Bank	14-08-1963
33.	Metropolitan Bank Ltd.	United Industrial Bank Ltd.	06-02-1964
34.	Cochin Nayar Bank Ltd.	State Bank of Travancore	08-02-1964
35.	Salem Shri Kannikaparameshwari Bank Ltd.	Karur Vysya Bank Ltd.	01-06-1964
36.	Uninaon Commercial Bank Ltd.	Bareilly Corporation Bank Ltd.	12-08-1964
37.	Latin Christian Bank Ltd.	State Bank of Travancore	17-08-1964
38.	Southern Bank Ltd.	United Industrial Bank Ltd.	24-08-1964
39.	Shri Jadeya Shankarling Bank Ltd.	Belgaum Bank Ltd.	26-10-1964

40.	Bareilly Bank Ltd.	Benarus State Bank Ltd.	16-11-1964
41.	Thiya Bank Ltd.	Lord Krishna Bank Ltd.	16-11-1964
42.	Allahabad Trading & Bkg. Corp. Ltd.	State Bank of India	25-08-1965
43.	Vettaikaran Padur Mahajan Bank Ltd.	Bank of Madura Ltd.	01-09-1965
44.	Malnad Bank Ltd.	State Bank of Mysore	06-10-1965
45.	Josna Bank Ltd.	Lord Krishna Bank Ltd.	13-10-1965
46.	Amrit Bank Ltd.	State Bank of Patiala	03-02-1968
47.	Chawla Bank Ltd.	New Bank of India	23-04-1969
48.	Bank of Behar Ltd.	State Bank of India	08-11-1969
49.	National Bank of Lahore Ltd.	State Bank of India	20-02-1970
50.	Miraj State Bank Ltd.	Union Bank of India	20-07-1985
51.	Lakshmi Commercial Bank Ltd.	Canara Bank	24-08-1985
52.	Bank of Cochin Ltd.	State Bank of India	26-08-1985
53.	Hindustan Commercial Bank Ltd.	Punjab National Bank	19-12-1986
54.	Traders Bank Ltd.	Bank of Baroda	13-05-1988
55.	United Industrial Bank Ltd.	Allahabad Bank	31-10-1989
56.	Bank of Tamilnad Ltd.	Indian Overseas Bank	20-02-1990
57.	Bank of Thanjavur Ltd.	Indian Bank	20-02-1990
58.	Parur Central Bank Ltd.	Bank of India	20-02-1990
59.	Purbanchal Bank Ltd.	Central Bank of India	29-08-1990
60.	New Bank of India	Punjab National Bank	04-09-1993

Some of the banks merged after the reform process started, are listed below:

Sr. No.	*Name of Bank Merged*	*With Whom Merged*	*Date of Merger*
61.	Bank of Karad Ltd.	Bank of India	1993-1994
62.	Kashinath Seth Bank	State Bank of India	1995-1996
63.	Punjab Co-op. Bank Ltd.	Oriental Bank of Commerce	1996-1997
64.	Bari Doab Bank Ltd.	Oriental Bank of Commerce	1996-1997
65.	Bareilly Corp. Bank Ltd.	Bank of Baroda	03-06-1999
66.	Sikkim Bank Ltd.	Union Bank of India	22-12-1999
67.	Times Bank Ltd.	HDFC Bank Ltd.	26-02-2000
68.	Benaras State Bank Ltd.	Bank of Baroda	20-07-2002
69.	Nedungadi Bank Ltd.	Punjab National Bank	01-02-2003
70.	Bank of Madura	ICICI Bank	Mar-2001
71.	Global Trust Bank Ltd.	Oriental Bank of Commerce	24-07-2004

This list is given as per information available. There are so many other banks which were merged but the names are not available. As per Table-2, 192 banks were merged from 1950 to 1964. As per above Table-1, banks merged after 1964 are 30, hence total number of banks merged from 1961 to 2004 comes to 192+30 = 222.

State of Saurashtra and State of Indore merged with SBI. Bank of Rajasthan merged with ICICI Bank Ltd. The Bank of Punjab merged with Centurian Bank Ltd. and Centurian Bank Ltd. was merged with HDFC Bank Ltd. recently.

Table: 2 Bank Mergers, Amalgamations and Transfer of Assets and Liabilities

Year	*Voluntary Amalgamations under Sec 44-A*	*Compulsory Merger under Sec 45*	*Other Mergers*	*Transfer of Assets and Liabilities*	*Total*
1950	4	-	-	-	4
1951	2	-	1	-	3
1952	-	-	4	-	4
1953	-	-	1	2	3
1954	-	-	-	1	1
1955	-	-	-	3	3
1956	-	-	-	-	-
1957	2	-	2	-	4
1958	4	-	2	1	7
1959	4	-	-	4	8
1960	2	-	-	5	7
1961	1	30	2	3	36
1962	3	1	2	5	11
1963	2	1	4	15	22
1964	7	9	1	62	79
Total	31	41	19	101	192

Source : 1 BA Bulletin Jan 2005.

33

Banking through Internet

E-Banking (also referred to as internet banking) is a generic name for the range of technologies that allow the exchange of information relating to banking transactions, electronically. It is becoming a strategic necessity for banks to conduct big volume and remmerative business. To be successful in e-banking, banks will have to build greater trust in their technological capability to ensure a demand driven regime rather than supply driven one.

The various components of e-banking are:

(a) Internet /Intranet/Extranet that use the web based technologies of graphical user interface to facilitate interaction and communication.

(b) Electronic data interchange which is an application of information using a standard format to structure the transaction of data.

(c) Electronic mail is exchange of mail messages by way of computer system connected over communication networking. These are sent and received at the user's convenience.

(d) Electronic fund transfer is the management of cash flow and timing of payments made to parties with the use of electronic messages.

(e) Smart card is credit sized plastic card with a computer chip embedded capable of storage of data and allowing it to be retrieved by a separate reader.

The components of e-banking are already available in banking sector but these are being used in isolation, which are required to be used in integrated banking software.

A combination of computers and communication technologies, at present, is enabling international banks and financial institutions to expand their reach and offer technology based product to a wide spectrum of clientele which was unthinkable in older days. The manufacturing, trading, service, Govt. organisations and home computer users may expect banks to use e-banking as a part of business.

An account holder in internet banking, having a password, can use internet banking for services like viewing operations in an account and credit card home loan balances, e-mail queries, feedback forms, order cheque book, stop payment of a cheque, accrued interest fees and taxes, transaction details of each account, pay bills, transfer funds to third party account etc.

How does the System Work?

A customer wanting to have internet banking transaction has to go to World Wide Web (www) for logging in the concerned website. The website service of concerned site verifies the ID and password and request are processed by the server. If the password and the ID match, the website permits the user to carry on the transaction. At the time of use of system, information about the transaction gets passed on the concerned bank which verifies account status and if it is found in order, the transaction is approved and carried.

Constraints

(a) Security remains to be a major issue in internet banking, especially for high transaction of corporate business. Various security options such as line encryption (a process through which a password, account information, transactions and other, transmitted information is scrambled so that no can figure out the key), branch connection encryption, fire-walls, digital certificates, automatic sign-offs, random pop-ups and disaster recovery sites are being looked at, to ensure that customer's money is safe in the cyber world.

(b) Verification of digital certificates is another major problem, for which a certificate authority is needed to be set up.

(c) The infrastructural cost of providing such services is quite high. A bank cannot automate its front-end systems to provide the robust function alone. It has to incur heavy expenditure for development of back-end system.

In a networked environment involving telecommunication lines, the computer security issues assume a more critical dimension and a well defined computer security and audit plan can ensure the long term success of IT plans of banks.

Advantages

The importance of traditional means of banking in distribution of banking services is likely to come down drastically over a period of time, with internet banking changing the business models, for major chunk of banking business. The advantages from e-banking could be as under:

1. The banks can use IT as a tool for designing and marketing aggressively a wide variety of retail banking products to capture the business of well-to-do customers in urban/metro centres. The customers in these centres expect faster remittance facilities, automatic teller machines and anywhere banking

facilities, telephone banking, home banking, credit card facility, personal loans including for car, houses, consumption purpose, cash management for corporate etc. The banks have started meeting these requirements of the customers.

2. Banks being essentially the processors of information in large quantities use the information technology (IT) to achieve the : (a) ability to handle larger volumes of business with desired level of efficiency (b) maximizing profitability of operations (c) exercising a strict vigil on costs.
3. The integration systems help by monitoring assets and liabilities movements and analysis of profit and loss and balance sheet details, tracing and monitoring, non-performing assets.
4. As per statistics available the transaction cost at ATM is 45 per cent of the cost across a bank counter while the cost of transaction in phone banking comes around 35 per cent, that of debit card 20 per cent and of internet merely 10 per cent. Hence, there could be substantial cost reduction of operations of banks.

Development in India

International banks have achieved certain objectives by using information technology in a big way while Indian banks have started entering recently in areas such as (a) collection, storage and processing of information in administrative offices (b) toning up book-keeping efficiency at branches by computerising back office operations (c) full branch computerisation (d) setting up automatic teller machines (ATMs).

To provide legal framework for electronic commerce and to enable electronic governance, the Govt. of India introduced the Cyber Bill-1999 in Lok Sabha on 16th Dec., 1999.

Several banks like SBI, PNB, ICICI Bank, UTI Bank (now Axis Bank); HDFC Bank, Global Trust Bank etc. have taken certain steps in recent past in the direction of providing banking services through internet. Foreign banks like Citi Bank or HSBC have also put certain systems for internet banking for its customers.

34

Real Time Gross Settlement System (RTGS)

Real time gross settlement system (RTGS) is a facility of Reserve Bank of India which allows both processing and final settlement of funds in real time.

With the increasing use of delivery channels for remitting funds, additional facility of RTGS—online has been implemented for all internet banking users of some big commercial banks. The Straight Through Processing (STP) facility allows interbank remittance in real time by entering minimum details and the beneficiary's account is credited without any manual intervention at the bank/branch. The facility allows both retail and corporate customers to initiate interbank remittances through concerned bank's internet banking channel by using RTGS mode.

By following few simple steps, internet banking user can imitate an inter-bank remittance just by click of a button. The transaction through internet banking channel can be initiated within the RBI stipulated time period, i.e., between 9.30 hrs to 14.45 hrs on working days and between 9.30 hrs to 11.45 hrs in Saturdays. RTGS transactions through internet banking channel are not permitted on Sundays, holidays and RBI declared RTGS holidays. Due to nature of real time settlement of transactions RTGS - online transactions can neither be scheduled nor can an advance-RTGS online transaction be initiated.

Once customer logs into internet banking services with a valid user-ID and password, he by clicking Bills/ RTGS would be able to initiate internet banking enabled RTGS transaction. The corporate internet banking customer has an additional facility for approving or recalling the RTGS initiated transaction.

RTGS - online offers following benefits to the internet banking customer:

1. Inter-bank remittance through internet.
2. Faster remittance–no waiting/no queues–funds transfer online.
3. Ease of operation and convenience.
4. Better cash management.
5. Low transaction cost.

By click of button from anywhere, within the stipulated time period and without any bank/branch intervention customers can now transfer funds from any RTGS enabled CBS (Centralised Banking Solutions) branch of some big banks to any RTGS enabled branch of other banks across the country.

The details of RTGS enabled branches of all banks is available on website of RBI (WWW.rbi.org.in) whereas details of concerned bank under CBS is available on concerned Banks website on internet banking services.

(*Source:* PNB Staff, Journal Vol. 48, No. 1, 2007).

35

Electronic Commerce: Application in Banking Sector

What is Electronic Commerce (E-commerce)?

Electronic commerce or E-commerce refers to paperless exchange of business information between organisations and individuals. E-commerce extends to any form of buying and selling by consumers and companies over a computer network. E-commerce includes Electronic Data Interchange (EDI), Electronic Mail, Electronic Bulletin Boards, Electronic Funds Transfer (EFT) and other technologies that are based on computer networks. The Buyer's Guide to Electronic commerce defines E-commerce as using information technology to improve relationship between partners.

E-commerce encompasses all forms of commercial transactions involving both organisations and individuals, that require the processing and transmission of digitized data including text, sound and visual images.

E-commerce is an emerging global reality that will have a significant impact on banking. It encompasses all three facets of contract of sale i.e. offer, acceptance and movement of consideration. The payment of money as on one leg of the transaction essentially involves banking. E-commerce is opening up new business possibilities and with the outreach of internet; it is expected to lead to a paradigm shift in the dynamics of business and banking. Today E-commerce is being seen as a single largest business window across the world.

In the past people used to exchange commodities depending upon their requirements and used to call it commerce. EC uses sophisticated computer technology, to conduct business transactions. It is a market place where business uses information technology and network computing to securely transform their business relationship, sell and buy goods and services and exchange information and data. EC addresses the need of organisations, merchants and consumers to cut costs, while improving the quality of goods and services and increasing the speed of service delivery. It allows people to transcend the barriers of time and distance and take advantage of global markets and business opportunities not even imaginable today, opening up new world of economic possibility and progress.

Advantages and Benefits of E-commerce

By automating manual processes and eliminating paper transactions EC facilitates the transaction of organisations from manual to a fully electronic environment, so as to change the way they operate with a view to improving their efficiency of operations.

There are three tangible benefits to the participants of EC activities as detailed below:

1. **Improvement in management of transactions:** EC minimises transaction cost by reducing the intermediation of third parties in putting through transactions. Transaction time is also reduced as the transaction is conducted electronically.
2. **Increase in business efficiency:** As EC lowers transaction costs, business efficiency also improves. EC allows electronic sharing of data between and

within organisations which can result in an improvement in products as well as processes. This leads to an increase in business efficiency.

3. **Development of new electronic markets:** EC creates business opportunities for the participants. For example, customers of certain banks that offer "internet banking" in India can now make payment online in respect of their electricity and telephone bills conveniently through their personal computers (PC). Customers can access services such as banking, insurance and travel reservations without stepping out their homes or offices. Such technological advances involving EC facilitate the development of new electronic markets.

Types of E-commerce

EC like any other normal business can be divided into three types:

1. Business to Consumer (B2C)
2. Business to Business (B2B)
3. Consumer to Consumer (C2C)

1. Business to Consumer (B2C): This is most popular and visible segment of EC. Here selling is not restricted to physical goods but also covers services and sale of information. Here the number of customers is large, but the per customer volume of transaction is low. Visibility of these sites is much higher than the other categories, as these sites do a lot of advertising both on and off the net. Here businesses directly sell to the end consumers. Thus, we have the concept of on-line shopping where you can now buy almost any product or service. Rediff.com, the most popular Indian B2C site, sells a range of products and claims a hit rate of 40 million every month. Sites like Rediff.com do not stock any items. The item a customer buys from these sites is redirected from the site to the suppliers affiliated to the sites and thus the order is placed with the suppliers, who send the item through courier. Here the courier company has a tie-up to deliver the goods on behalf of EC site.

Under this segment, EC is going to have a significant impact on information intensive and service oriented industries, such as financial services and ICE (Information, Communication and Entertainment). Products which are basically of an impulsive buying nature are the first ones to move to the net. Thus, books, music, chocolates, flowers, making airline/hotel reservations etc. were the first on the net Amazon.com is the most famous site worldwide, where you can buy almost any book online.

2. Business to Business (B2B): In this type of EC, businesses sell and buy from other businesses e.g. Intel sells its chips to other businesses–OEM's who make computers. Many large companies are using EC in some way or the other. They have started B2B transactions with suppliers. In this scenario, we have a limited number of customers but the transaction amounts per transaction are large. Samsung has redefined its business paradigm, and deployed EC to redefine its critical business process linking if, directly to its suppliers distributors. The big 3 automakers of USA–GM, Ford and Diamler Chrysler announced plans to channel their on-line supply, buying through a single internet portal, creating the world's largest virtual market-place. An idea of the size of this market can be gauged by the fact that the Big 3 spends $240 billion on supplies annually. Besides auto maker's supplier groups spend another $500 billion annually.

3. Consumer to Consumer (C2C): This type of EC is not very common at present. Most visible examples are auction sites. If one has something to sell, then you can get listed to an auction site and others scan bid for it. The auction site e-bay.com has bought the concept of virtual auction to the C2C space.

The other emerging areas of EC are e-governance with basic idea of having smart (simple, moral, accountable, reliable, and transparent) government for improving processes for tax-collection, revenue and resource management, effective deployment of funds. This could be achieved by B2G (Business-to-Government) and G2C (government to consumer) EC. Thus areas like fling of IT returns, payment of bills/dues, licenses, records of land revenue, sale documents, issue of certificates and licenses etc. could be covered.

E-commerce in India is at nascent stage but will grow quickly on account of the positive and encouraging developments that are taking place in the industry, such as framing of comprehensive cyber-law, setting up of national digital certification authority, providing global level telecom infrastructure with competitive tariffs and permitting private internet service providers to set up gateways. It is noticed that the Credit Rating Information Services of India Limited (CRISIL) has signed an MOU with Satyam Infoway to provide performance capability ratings and financial ratings of B2B, EC participants. Slowly but surely, EC is making the banking industry seamless. Banks can reap the benefits of participation in EC. In this regard the participation and experience gained by banks operating in "wired" countries such as USA, UK and Japan, would be a good point of reference for Indian banks, proposing to enter the EC arena.

36

Trading On-line through Internet

Information and communication technology is fast becoming the backbone of financial and economic sector in India and world over. Information technology has played an important role not only to complete the activity with high efficiency but also has become a potential driver to ubnovate and meet future requirements.

Technology in financial sector has made customer feel comfortable and relaxed to undertake financial transactions over internet world over. The use of various electronic and telecommunication networks have set a sound platform for delivering a wide range of added products and services.

One of the latest benefits internet offers is on-line share trading without any manual intervention of any level. The facility offers a complete electronic for dealing in capital market in India and worldwide.

With the changing scenario and use to electronic means in settlement of payment and shares, the time taken in settling a deal has reduced considerably. The benefit online share trading offers is timely settlement and complete transparency in the complete trading cycle.

An online share trading mechanism can be offered when broker, banker and depository join hands through combination of information and communication technology and make available a user friendly convenient environment to the investor/customers for trading in securities.

The customer/ investor are required to open three types of accounts to enjoy the benefits of hassle-free online share trading:

1. Trading account with broker.
2. Demat account with depository.
3. Payment account with bank.

The settlement of shares is done as per the laid down guidelines of SEBI:

Benefits of Online Share Trading to Customers/Banks

Customers	*Banks*
1. Convenience of trading online.	1. Value added services
2. Online access any day from anywhere	2. Attracting new customers due to prompt and good services
3. Online monitoring of all accounts	3. All information in electronic mode.
4. Trading any share	4. Revenue generation for the bank concerned
5. Online information on share prices	5. No manual intervention transaction online
6. No manual intervention of bank/broker	6. Reduction in cost in handling cash, cheque, drafts, etc.
7. No limit on trading online	

37

A Sea Change in Banking Sector in India after Independence

Banks perform a very critical role of financial intermediation is accepting the deposits from the savers (public) and lending to needy persons is borrowers, and in the process facilitate efficient allocation of funds. In their role as financial intermediaries, banks undertake transformation of risk size and maturity and play a catalytic role in the economic growth. Banks are a critical link in the transmission mechanishm of monetary policy and enable efficient transmission of policy actions. Thus banks play a very important role in the overall economy of the country.

Banking in India has a long history and its evolution makes an interesting case study. It has evolved over a period into a resilient system and has received international acclaim for surviving the Global crisis with any major impact.

The present banking structure in India consists of commercial banks, Urban cooperative banks, regional rural banks (RRBs) and rural cooperative banks, which, in turn comprise short term cooperative credit structural/state cooperative banks and district central cooperative banks and long term credit structure (State cooperative agriculture and rural development banks and primary cooperative agriculture and rural development banks). Commercial banks form the bedrock of the Indian financial system accounting for a significant portion of the total assets.

This Chapter tracks the evolution of Indian commercial banking with a corresponding recounting of evolution of its regulation.

Evolution of Banking in India

Evolution of banking in India can be categorised into three major phases the early phase (1947-67), the phase of social controls (1967-1991) and the reform phase (1991 onwords).

Banking in the Early years of Independent India : 1947-1967

At the time of independence, Indian baking sector was under developed, lacking in depth. Banks were owned by the private sector and as such there was large concentration of resources mobilised through deposits in the hands of a few business families like TATA, Birla, Dalmia etc. As a result, the credit requirements of agriculture and other needy sectors were ignored. The early phase of banking development was characterized by three fundamental milestone developments: enactment of Banking companies Act, 1949 (Later renamed as the Banking Regulation Act), the deposit Insurance Corporation Act 1961 and the nationalization of the Imperial Bank of India in 1955. The focus of these developments was to put in place an enabling legal framework capable of ushering in bank regulation, protection to depositor and extension of banking facilities on a large-scale more particularly in rural and semi-urban areas, through the New Branch Licensing Policy (1962). Reflecting these developments, population per branch fell significantly from 1,36,000 in 1951 to 65000 in 1967.

Social Control over Banks 1967-1991

Despite the expansion of banking network, the share of agriculture in credit dispensed by scheduled commercial banks remained stagnant, In order to enhance the spread of banks credit, the concept of social control over banking sector was introduced. The main objective of social control was to achieve a wider spread of bank credit, prevent its misuse, direct a larger volume of credit flow to priority sectors and to make it an effective instrument of economic development. Nationalisation of banks was resorted to in 1969 (14 banks and subsequently 6 banks in 1980). Introduction of specific schemes like Lead Banks Scheme (LBS) and Service Area Approach (SAA) were other policy initiatives characterising the phase. This phase also witnessed institutional development in the form of setting up of Regional Rural Banks (RRBs) aimed at meeting the credit needs of small and marginal farmers.

This phase was, however, marked by significant expansion of the Governments budget and increased statutory preemptions (as high as 63.5%) of banks resources to finance high fiscal deficits. The proliferation of directed credit arrangements, administered interest rates and increase in statutory preemptions, all had an adverse impact on bank's profitability and capital base.

Phase of Financial Sector Reforms 1991 onwards

Comprehensive reform measures were undertaken in 1991 in the wake of Balance of payments crisis, encompassing trade, external and banking sectors. The objective of the banking sector reforms was to promote diversified, efficient and competitive financial system with the ultimate objective of improving the allocative efficiency of resources through operational flexibility, improved financial viability and institutional strengthening. The reforms have focused on removing financial repression through reductions in statutory preemptions, while setting up and aligning prudential regulations to the international standards (Basel 1) and benchmarks in a phased manner. Furthermore, interest rates on both deposits and advances of banks have been progressively deregulated. The banking sector reforms essentially took a two pronged approach. First, the level of competition was gradually increased within the banking system while simultaneously interdicting international best practices in prudential regulation and supervision tailored to Indian requirements. Second, active steps were taken to improve the institutional arrangements including the legal framework and technological system.

Measures to improve the health of banking system have included (i) restoration of public sector banks net worth through recapitalisation, (ii) streamlining of the supervision process with combination of on-site and off- site surveillance along with external auditing (iii) introduction of structured and discretionary intervention for problem banks through a prompt corrective action (PCA) mechanism; (iv), institutionalisation of mechanism facilitating greater coordination for regulation and supervision of financial conglomerates; (v) strengthening of creditor rights (still in process); and (vi) increased emphasis on corporate governance.

On the back of concerted policy efforts, the banking sector performance has improved over the years, especially during the post-reform period. Gross Non-performing Assets (NPAs) as percentage of gross advances fell from 15.7 per cent as at end march 1997 to 2.9 per cent as at-end march 2012 while return on assets (ROA) improved from 0.81 per cent to 1.07 per cent during the same period. The capital Adequacy Ratio (CAR) remained above 10 per cent from end march 1997 and above 12 per cent from end march 2002. It reached 14.1 per cent as at end March 2012 (Source Youjana Jan 2013).

Overseas presence of Indian banks has also gone up considerably during this period and currently there are 165 branches of Indian banks operating overseas. Consistent with the policy approach to benchmark the banking system to the best international standards with emphasis on gradual harmonisation, all commercial banks (except Local Area

Banks and RRBs) migrated to BASEL II framework by March, 2009.

Evolution of Bank Regulation in India

A robust regulatory framework is a prerequisite for the development of banking system. Prior to 1949, the banking companies, along with other companies, were governed by the Indian Companies Act, 1913. This Act, however contained very few provisions specifically applicable to banks. There were also a few ad hoc enactments, such as the Banking companies (Inspection) Ordinace, 1946, and the Banking Companies (Restriction of Branches) Act, 1946, covering specific regulatory aspects. There was no separate legislative framework for regulation of the banking system.

In march 1949, a special legislation, called the Banking companies Act 1949, applicable exclusively to the banking companies was passed. This Act was renamed as the Banking Regulation Act in March 1966. The Act vested in the Reserve Bank of India, the responsibility relating to licensing of banks, branch expansion, liquidity of their assest, management and methods of working, amalgamation, reconstruction and liquidation. Various amendments in several provisions of the Act were made from time to time addressing the evolving imperatives of the banking sector developments.

The overarching philosophy underlying banking regulation in India has been to ensure that the growth of financial sector remains in alignment with the growth of real sector and that there is a harmonised development of real and financial sectors. While recognising the significance of innovation for effient allocation of resources and increased competition, the regulation adopted a measured approach, striking a balance between cost of misadventures and benefits of growth. In recognition of Indian regulatory approach, RBI was awarded the 2012 "Dufrenoy prize" for facilitating responsible innovation in finance.

Indian Banking Regulation during the Global Crisis

The recent global financial crisis which wreaked great havoc in the international financial landscape, fortunately, did not have any significant impact on the Indian Banking system. This was mainly due to the fact that the Indian banking system had negligible exposure to toxic assets, did not have exotic structured products and, more importantly, had in place a micro prudential frame work which addressed the procyclicality and interconnected dimensions of the systemic risk.

The Developments in the Indian financial regulation in the post – Crisis period, therefore, have, primarily been guided by the immediate imperative of containing the financial contagion from abroad and carrying forward the process of financial sector reforms in a calibrated manner distilling the lessons from the crisis and aligning the regulatory and supervisory framework to the evolving international standards (Basel III) in the wake of the Crisis.

To cushion the adverse impact on India, of the global economic downturn, many measures were undertaken. The sector-specific counter-cyclical regulatory measures (reduction in risk-weights and provisioning) were undertaken in conjuction with the easing of the monetary policy measures. Considering the tightness in the market liquidity as the immediate impact of global crisis, adequate liquidity, both rupee and forex, was ensured. Rupee liquidity was augmented through measures including progressive reduction in Cash reserve Ratio (CRR) and policy rates and by providing a special repo window under Liquidity Adjustment Facility (LAF) for banks for on lending to Non-bank Financial companies (NBFCS). Housing Finance Companies (HFCS) and mutual funds. Measures for augmenting forex liquidity in the banking system comprised upward revision of interest rate ceilings on Non-Resident deposits; relaxation of External Commercial Borrowings (ECB) regime; allowing BNFCS/ HFCs access to external borrowings and introduction of rupee-dollar swap facility for banks with overseas branches to provide comfort in managing short term funding needs.

The regulatory measures initiated for furthering financial sector reforms could broadly be classified into those aimed at strengthening resilience of the financial system and these aimed at institutional and market development. Measures under the former included implementation of advanced approaches of Basel II and Basel III, while the later comprised development of market for securitisation and CDS, setting up of Financial Stability Development Council (FSDC), proposal for the introduction of holding company structure for banks, proposal for granting additional licenses for entry of new banks in private sector and deregulation of interest rates on savings deposits.

